The Fear of 13

The Fear of 13

Nick Yarris

CENTURY

1 3 5 7 9 10 8 6 4 2

Century
20 Vauxhall Bridge Road
London SW1V 2SA

Century is part of the Penguin Random House group of companies whose
addresses can be found at global.penguinrandomhouse.com

First published by Century in 2016

www.penguin.co.uk

A CIP catalogue record for this book is available from the British Library.

ISBN 9781780896526 (trade paperback)

Typeset in Baskerville MT Std (12.5 /17.8 pt) by Thomson Digital Pvt Ltd, Noida, Delhi
Printed and bound in Great Britain by Clays Ltd, St Ives plc

Penguin Random House is committed to a sustainable future for
our business, our readers and our planet. This book is made
from Forest Stewardship Council® certified paper.

For Jayne and Michael Yarris

Contents

Preface

First, let me say hello, and I'd really appreciate it if you would say hello back. Simply put, for the first two years of my prison ordeal I couldn't say hello to anyone without a prison officer giving me a whack across the face for doing this otherwise simple act. An act which violated the 'silence rule' I was made to live under on Death Row.

Because I was made to endure such a humiliation, I ask every audience that I now speak before to simply say hello back to me as I feel I have paid so dearly to earn that from them. For me it's my way to hold my head up in the face of being so cowed in life. I hope that by the time you finish this book, you will offer me as much in respect for what it took for me to come back from such a hell to say this same thing to you here in these pages . . .

1 Down the path

If I had only known what was waiting for me I would never have gone down that path that day when I was seven years old. Yet if I had *really* known what was being offered to me in my life right now, then I'd like to think that maybe, just maybe, I would have had the courage to go through it all again . . .

Until the age of seven, I had a really normal life, I guess. I was a happy, contented little boy, growing up with my mom and dad and my five siblings on a friendly little street in a family neighbourhood on the edge of south-west Philadelphia.

My father, Michael Yarris Senior, met and fell in love with my mother, Harriet 'Jayne' Shaw, in 1957 when they were both living in an area of old Philadelphia called The Meadows. My father was a second-generation Russian-American and my mother third-generation Irish-English. Together they raised our family in one of the three-bedroom 'row homes' that made up many of the mostly new immigrant neighbourhoods sown throughout Philadelphia.

At the time my life changed for ever, my eldest sister Nettie was twelve, Anna Marie was ten and Mabel 'Sissy' was nine; then there were my brothers, Michael 'Mikey' Yarris Jr who was eight and Martin 'Marty', aged four. Our family dog at the time was a 14 lb black poodle named Jocko who had decided that I was his best friend in the whole world – and I agreed. Wherever I went, he shadowed my every move. It really was as blissful as that, with Jocko and me innocently discovering life together, and finding that it was wonderful.

Although I can no longer exactly recall the child that I was before the attack, I do have some clear memories of those early years. They also provided me with something tangible to hold on to through the really dark days of what was to come; they became a sort of 'beacon' for me to home in on as I fought my way back to becoming once again that person I had begun my life as.

In particular I have a wonderful photograph from this time, taken during a family vacation. It is a picture of my big brother Mikey and me. We were so close then, I swear he was the greatest big brother to have. There I am, wearing these 'Chuck Taylor' low-top basketball trainers which he had given me and which I prized above anything else. They were all frayed and washed out from having been put through the laundry so many times, and even the rivets on the sides were gone. They were also too big for me. But I was so pleased because I was no longer wearing 'Pro-keds', which were for babies.

But these weren't just hand-me-downs; Mikey had given me these shoes of his as a form of protection, to stop me being teased by some of the other children. He saw them as his chance to step in and do what a great older brother does: stand up for me.

The events that were to change my life for ever began in the spring of 1968, which was one really wild year in America's history. From the assassination of Dr Martin Luther King Jr in April to the assassination of Vice-President Robert F. Kennedy in June, and on through to the summer riots in cities all over America, it was a very scary year for us all. The country was in the middle of the Vietnam War and also the Apollo space race against Russia. As a child just waking up to all that was going on in the world, it really was an important time to witness.

To me, it seemed as if each new day brought some earth-shattering news of ever bigger and scarier things that were changing the world. I wonder how many other people my age remember being shown how to curl up under our desks in class each morning in order to 'practise' our protection manoeuvres in the event of nuclear war. Every day at Patterson Elementary School, having pledged our allegiance to our country, we had to put our hands over our heads and curl up real small under our desks in case the Cubans fired nuclear missiles at us. We were told that the metal desks would protect us from falling debris and that we had to stay there until they sounded the safety note over the emergency public address system. The adult world was crazy.

This particular day, though, started like any other. I was just a little boy in third grade who'd been given an unexpected day off school and my imagination was filled with all the fun and freedom that such freedom brings. It all began when my black poodle Jocko and I were walking along a footpath in the woods near our home. I think I had gone to a dental appointment that morning and had returned home with my mother, rather than going back to school, and I was filled with that sweet boyish feeling of bursting free.

I still recall how my mother shouted at me not to get my school clothes dirty and to stay away from the creek which ran behind our home as I sped out of the front door with Jocko yipping happily at my heels.

Paying no heed to my mother's customary warnings, I was off on one of the many adventures I shared with Jocko. We were on our way from the creek towards the open field where we both knew there were rabbits for Jocko to chase and places for me to hide and pretend to be a hunter on the loose.

That was when I saw him, sitting on the roof of a small wooden structure made by some local teenagers out of scrap wood. We were only about fifty yards from some houses but this home-made 'fort' was half hidden among some small shrubs and trees. I knew I wasn't supposed to be here, as it was out of sight of the adults, but once I noticed he'd seen me I tried to act brave and continue on my way past the boy sitting on the fort.

He waited for me to get right up to the small clearing in the path leading up to where he was perched, then he jumped down easily from his position and stood in front of me, a lit cigarette hanging from the corner of his mouth. I knew who he was because he lived in the street adjoining mine and I had watched as he earned his place in the local pecking order for his street fighting. He was a member of a gang of boys ten or twelve years older than me who hung around the neighbourhood drinking beer. He had a reputation for violence and I was really intimidated by him as I'd previously seen him assault grown-ups as well as other children. Why would he waste his time talking to me? I wondered.

I had no idea what to expect as he stood there looking down at me. He held the cigarette out to me and although I shook my head, he just ignored me and pushed the lit end right near my face as I instinctively backed away. Then he ordered me to take the cigarette and puff on it.

I tried to do as he said but I got it all wrong, I didn't inhale. He told me to try again. I was so scared and my hand shook so badly that when I took my second puff I dropped the cigarette. Even though Jocko was yelping and growling at the boy, I could tell my Jocko was afraid, too. Then I began coughing. My head became filled with fog as the smoke filled my lungs and I began to lose focus.

The next memory I have is of lying on my back looking up at the leaves on the trees through the branches. I'm not in any pain but I'm not altogether awake either. Then I feel the uneven ground under my lower back and his hands on my chest as he roughly twists my shoulders round to align with his. His hand covers both my mouth and my nose, and

I start to panic as I fight for breath. He smiles weirdly as he nearly leaves his hand there too long. I choke wildly as he finally pulls it off.

By this time I am in such a panic that I begin to pee myself. Which just enrages him further as he lifts himself up from me. That's when I look up again and see the stone in his right hand. He brings it towards my head and the next thing I hear is a wet smack. My eyes go red, then black. I lose consciousness to the sounds of the high-pitched angry noise that he makes as he finally finishes raping me.

I have no idea how long I was out for but I was moaning as I came round to hear him hiss in my ear, 'Shut up! Shut the fuck up!' I felt my eyes with my left hand. The lids were swollen nearly shut. As I tried to sit up he knelt on my shoulders, his knees either side of my head, and pinned me there, saying all these things I didn't understand.

At one moment he sounded nearly hysterical, almost crying and pleading as he told me the things I would have to say were the causes of my injuries; in the next he switched to rage and anger, hissing dire threats that all spewed out on top of each other. When he had composed himself some, he started to tell me how he would kill Jocko and my entire family if I told anyone what had happened. Then there was this moment when he seemed to be deciding whether he had scared me enough to keep me silent. At last he ran off and left me.

My head was in such a haze as I tried to find my way back home that, even though it was so close, I kept getting lost as I screamed and screamed for Jocko to come until my lungs burned. I knew I'd be in trouble with Mom for going where I wasn't supposed to go and for ruining my clothes, and I was sure I was going to get a whipping if my parents ever found out about the cigarette.

When I eventually reached our front door, Mom saw me and nearly fainted. There was a huge bruise across my forehead where I had been hit by the stone and my eyes were nearly swollen shut. I told her that I had fallen over and she was so alarmed by my appearance that she never questioned how or where I had fallen. She immediately called for an ambulance, which took me to a specialist eye hospital, the Wills Eye Institute in south Philadelphia. The doctors were concerned that the continued swelling would cause brain damage or that my eyesight might be affected, but following treatment I was released later that day.

That evening, when my father asked me what had happened, I told him I had been walking along a wall pushing a shopping cart when it had tipped over and taken me with it; I'd fallen on to the cart and banged my head, I said. It was the lie the boy who'd attacked me had told me to tell anyone who asked.

It was also the first step to the lie that not only kept me trapped by what he had done to me but which he would use to bind me to him in secrecy for several years to come.

I now wish with all my heart – for myself and for my family – that I had spoken out about the attack right away. No matter what I had done wrong – by going where I wasn't supposed to go and by smoking a cigarette – I should have told my parents what had happened. But it was the weapon that he used on me every time he saw me alone. I hated it that from this time onwards for the next few years he would catch me by myself in an alley and just scare the hell out of me, before roughing me up a little as a reminder of how much bigger and stronger than me he was. I would hide in our basement and just pummel my fists into my legs because my head was all confused and I wanted to fight him but I felt so weak. There was nothing I could do, and the longer I kept silent, the less likely it was that anyone would believe me.

By the time I was ten or eleven it was like I could never convince anyone that the attack was real any more. I had also convinced myself that if I had not been so weak and afraid that day he would not have attacked me. There must have been something about me sexually that had made him attack me, I felt. Was it because I didn't look masculine enough? I found myself trying harder and harder to be stronger and more masculine in any way I could. I wanted to be able to fight so that I could protect myself. I wanted to be menacing like him so that people would fear me.

Unknowingly, all the things inside me that had made me the person I was, left me after the attack, to be replaced by a chaos of violence and uncontrolled behaviour. School changed from being a wonderful place that I attended eagerly in order to learn, to this mad world where even my ability to see written words had changed.

The physical damage to my brain had two effects: the curvature of my eyes altered and my ability to see words correctly was also affected. Soon I was the child with the behavioural problems who was always being taken out of class for acting up.

Meanwhile, the seeds of dysfunction already sown amongst my five siblings were growing with every passing year. It was as if this unique era in America's history was also pitched against my family. Racial violence and rampant drug use were the two common themes of my childhood. My whole family was as deeply affected by this as any other. But I was also growing up at a time when whole cities were being set on fire in race riots, and Philadelphia was no exception. Those were tumultuous times, as America went to war with itself, and it was all too easy for the system to overlook the psychological problems of a little white kid in a nondescript section of Philadelphia.

With my secret driving me deeper and deeper into self-abuse, it seemed that I was set on a sure path to self-destruction. I drank beer for the first time at the age of ten. This was at a family celebration and, after a few sips, I felt as if I had left every fear or worry behind at last. From then on, I wanted to feel the same way that beer made me feel all the time. By the age of fourteen I was using drugs or alcohol every day.

At fifteen I was arrested for the first time – for stealing from a neighbour's home to purchase drugs. Then, after I was arrested and placed in a juvenile hospital facility, in a fit of panic I stuck my fingers in an electric fan, nearly cutting them off. By this time it should have been clear to any adult that I had emotional and developmental problems, but, despite my early arrest, the system did not catch up with me.

Upon my release from hospital I was placed in a school for troubled children, but before I had completed my senior year I was arrested again for petty crimes. As my life continued to spiral out of control it seemed as if all anyone said to me was: 'You're going to be dead or doing life in prison by the time you're twenty-one.'

It became a self-fulfilling prophecy that I could feel pulling me along.

2 The wrong path and no directions

I went from a childhood ruled by a terrible secret to a chaotic adolescence addled by drugs and alcohol abuse. All of which meant I had no real chance of living a normal life and I can admit now how much I hated myself for how I felt inside. It showed in how I acted and how I spoke. It was as if I was not able to be who I wanted because of what had been done to me – so why not just tear my whole life to shreds?

Through my teenage years I was becoming adrift and losing any real chance to address the damage caused to my brain by the attack on me when I was seven. Many of the mental functions of which most other adults are capable were beyond me. I had an overwhelming need for instant gratification and an impulse control disorder that impaired my ability to wait for even the most basic things in life. In conversations I would just speak over what other people were saying. My brain never slowed enough to allow me this simple patient act. In times of severe stress it would kind of shut down and I would become temporarily unable either to communicate myself or to understand what was being said to me. This disorder, known medically as aphasia, affects the frontal lobe area of the brain responsible for speech process and reasoning.

With drugs soon dominating my daily life, my behaviour was becoming too much for my parents to deal with. After I was involved in a violent fight with my brothers in which the house was extensively damaged, they reached breaking point and when I was eighteen they kicked me out of the family home. Being homeless and abusing both alcohol and drugs, I found myself in an inevitable downward spiral. My drug of choice was methamphetamine, a form of purified home-made speed, the effect of which was to calcify the frontal lobe of my brain, and therefore send me further out of control. Soon the drugs were having a profound effect on me. I began to suffer increasingly from headaches and sleep deprivation, to the point where reasoning became near impossible and my behaviour more and more erratic. Once, my parents found me sleeping in their car with a gun in my belt and muttering that I was being 'hunted'. They were both afraid *of* me and *for* me. And they were afraid that I had lost my mind to the drugs.

Manufactured by street gangs in Philadelphia, methamphetamine, or 'meth' as it was known, was cheap to purchase. A potent narcotic with the ability to last twelve hours per use, it was destroying the lives of thousands of young people just like me. I would go on what were called 'meth binges', in which I would also stay up drinking all night then go for days with little or no sleep.

During one particular binge in October 1980, I stole a car and drove it for three days to Florida. On 11 November 1980 I destroyed a hotel room in Miami Beach and was arrested and then hospitalised by the authorities for the incident. I spent the next eight months in the South Florida State Mental Hospital. It was here, though, that I was finally diagnosed with aphasia and underwent some treatment.

Following my release from hospital, I pleaded guilty to the criminal charges I faced in Florida and was sent back to Pennsylvania to face charges for the crimes I had committed there.

Once I was in custody back in Philadelphia, my parents decided they would help me as they believed that the treatment I had received at the hospital back in Florida had given me the chance to get clean and start my life over. They raised enough bail money to have me released on bond and, at the age of twenty, I was allowed to live at home for the first time since I'd been kicked out over two years previously.

Then, in September 1981, I got a job as a sales clerk in a retail store in central Philadelphia. For a while my life seemed stable. Finally off drugs for the first time in years, I began to try and mend the family ties that had been so strained over the years. I also met a girl named Teresa, whom I began to date regularly. As 1981 came to an end, my life was the best it had been for a long time. The deterioration in my brain had slowed and, since being informed that I was affected by a real disorder, I learned to control it.

If I stayed away from 'speed', the aphasia would not progress any further. Yet sadly, this only sober period of my adult life to date was to prove fleeting. It wasn't long before I broke up with my girlfriend and went right back to drinking and doing drugs. In the span of just two weeks my life slipped back into a black hole of hate and anger. I quit my job and began to stay away from home for days at a time. And just like that, I lost nearly every sound foothold I had in my life.

Once again I fell out with my parents. They were simply overwhelmed by so many factors. They were both out of work and the family was bordering on bankruptcy. At this point things began to unravel even further.

My older brother Mikey had also suffered brain damage at the age of eighteen, when he had fallen from the top of a commercial building while working as a roofer with my father. As a result of this he had undergone open brain surgery which had left him with a complete personality change and he too had become an alcoholic and a drug user. Not only that, but my younger brother Marty had become an alcoholic and drug addict as well. The toxic mix of so many family members doing drugs and drinking on a daily basis led to constant upheaval in the household. When not staying away for days doing drugs, I returned to the family home only to shower or change clothing. This always brought renewed turmoil and fighting. It seemed that something had to give.

In the early morning hours of 4 December 1981, I was stopped by the local police while driving a stolen car through the centre of Philadelphia high on drugs. I tried to run away and they had to chase me through several city blocks, but they eventually caught up with me and gave me a beating. I was left with nearly 200 stitches in my lip and mouth where I had been struck in the teeth with a club by one of the officers. I was charged with resisting arrest, possession of a stolen car and assault. Only after having seen what physical damage the police had done to my mouth did my family pay for me to be bailed out, and I was again released to my parents' custody to await the outcome of these new criminal charges.

At home, mostly hiding in my bedroom nursing two broken teeth and my slowly healing wounds, I sank into depression. The endless cycle of my day-to-day life seemed bleaker than ever and it was only a matter of time before I was back behind the wheel of another car I had stolen to pay for drugs.

It was at this point, caught up in the mess of my life and feeling like I was barely holding things together, that on 19 December 1981, while driving through the streets of Chester, Pennsylvania at 2 a.m., my life took another lurch.

I was pulled over by a patrol car driven by one Officer Benjamin Wright for going through a stop sign. As I saw the police car with its flashing red and blue lights, I started to panic. That panic mixed badly with the narcotics already swilling around my brain and I could feel my mind shutting down. Sitting behind the wheel of the car, waiting for the officer to approach me, I froze with fear.

When the officer reached my car he began to speak to me through its open window but I couldn't answer. My brain was fighting the rush of adrenaline and I simply could not say anything. Which really seemed to annoy the officer. I must have appeared detached, uncommunicative and intoxicated. He opened the driver's door and placed his hand on my shoulder, but I just sat there staring up at him. Then I simply stood up. The officer tried to place a resisting hand on my shoulder again, but to no effect. That angered him – he was a big man used to being able to control others physically. He grabbed me by the shirtfront and braced me against the car's side with his forearm against my throat, shouting at me to stand still, but I didn't hear or understand what he was shouting.

Inside my adrenaline-rushed, drug-addled brain everything seemed to unfold in slow motion. I pushed away his hand, like a parent sweeping away a child's hand from their trouser leg. Even though I had movement, no matter how hard I tried, I could not speak the words I was ordering my brain to say.

In reality events were happening quickly as Officer Wright soon became fearful of this young man who was quite out of control.

He grabbed his club from his belt and raised it to strike me. But looking up, I simply reached out and took it from him with a swift yank that left him outraged. Next he took his pistol from its holster and, just as he did so, I grabbed his wrist. Instantly we became locked in a fight for control of the gun.

Inevitably, the gun discharged and everything came to a halt. It seemed as if the whole world went silent.

'OK! OK!' I began yelling loudly, over and over, as the gunshot from the officer's gun also sent him back to reality.

I yelled 'OK' again, to show that I was now surrendering fully.

The shaken officer placed his gun to my chin and flung me into the patrol car's protected rear seat area before slamming the door shut. Then, after composing himself for a moment while sitting in the front seat, Officer Wright made a decision. He lifted the car radio to his mouth and began calling for back-up on the police radio, yelling: '*Shots fired! Officer assist! Shots fired! Officer assist!*'

I was shocked that he did this when there was nothing going on physically between him and me. He smiled at me in the rear-view mirror as he set down the radio. I knew my life as I had known it was over.

Sitting in the back of that patrol car, the accumulation of all the events of the previous few years seemed to collide in my mind, as if the complete lack of control in my life had finally come to its inevitable conclusion. Everything seemed to pile up on me at once and I began to cry uncontrollably.

Meanwhile, Officer Wright was outraged and shaken – and in the moments between his making his emergency request and the time the back-up police officers arrived on the scene, my fate was sealed, and my life changed for ever. Because, when his fellow officers finally arrived, Officer Benjamin Wright decided to tell them that I had attempted to kill him. That was why he had smiled at me in the rear-view mirror.

I was shocked as I listened to him say how it was a miracle he had survived the attack at all, as I had taken his gun from him, then tried to shoot him in the face before he'd managed to wrestle it from me. His fellow officers looked at me like I was scum and they did not hesitate to inflict a rough trip to the local police station, where I was charged with the kidnapping, aggravated assault and attempted murder of Officer Wright.

When I was brought before a judge for a bail hearing on the attempted murder charges, I was informed by the public defender who stood beside me that, if convicted, I faced a minimum of twenty years in prison, but more likely I was looking at a life sentence.

I was sent to Delaware County jail to be held for court and, because the charges against me were so serious, I was placed in solitary confinement. Regardless of whether or not the charges were true, the reality was that I very probably did face a life in prison for the foreseeable future.

In the days that followed my arrest I simply fell apart. I went through 'cold turkey' (the prison service offered no withdrawal treatments for drug addicts in 1981) and sank into a depression that bordered on suicidal.

It was as I sat alone in my cell trying to imagine a way out of my situation that I came up with the most desperate plan of all. I somehow arrived at the idea that if I had information about a huge unsolved crime then the police would make a deal with me and would let me go. This single thought became a ray of light in the darkness of my life, the one thing to keep me from falling apart or giving up completely.

But what information did I have? I was pretty much a loner, so no one confided in me, and what did I know anyway? Then my eyes fell on the story of an unsolved murder in the local paper which had been sitting in my cell when I'd arrived.

Linda Mae Craig, a 33-year-old mother of three, had been abducted from the local Tri-State shopping mall car park in her own car, then raped and stabbed to death. The car had been dumped near a big road intersection and her body had been found buried in the snow in the parking lot of nearby Chester Baptist Temple Church. I had read the story a hundred times over before, but now I was searching for any little detail that I could use to help get me out of here. Slowly, the workings of a plan began to form in my mind.

After all, what did I have to lose? I'd been told to expect a prison sentence of twenty years or more for the attempted murder of a police officer and, realistically, what jury was going to accept the word of a confirmed drug addict and thief against that of a police officer?

I was alone and afraid, and this new reality I now found myself in was bizarre and scary. But what I did next was pure madness.

3 What goes around comes around

Back in December 1979, I'd shared a house for a few weeks with a man named Jimmy Brisbois. He and I were drug buddies and we'd been hanging around together. When my parents threw me out for my bad behaviour I'd moved in with him to help pay the rent.

One day while I was living there, I broke into a car and stole a collection of silver coins. At that time in America, silver and gold were very expensive commodities and it turned out that the coins were worth around $5,000. But I should have known better than to tell Jimmy about the coins, because a few hours later he and another man beat me up in the apartment and knocked me unconscious. I had gone out to the store to get some groceries, and when I came back in the door they'd hit me from behind with something hard that had knocked me senseless. Then they'd taken everything I had and wrapped my unconscious body in a rug, tied a rope around it and dumped me in the snow about five miles from Jimmy's house, behind a large warehouse out by the Delaware river. Having left me there for dead they had taken the coins and disappeared.

It was dark and freezing cold when a man who was walking to his car in the rear of the parking lot found me an hour or two later struggling to get out of the rug. He probably saved my life. He cut the cord around the rug and I crawled out, a bloody mess. This 60-year-old black man had just finished work when he found me and he wanted to call an ambulance or the police, but I told him to leave me alone. I walked back to my neighbourhood that night filled with rage.

Then I went looking for Jimmy and the other man, with a gun I had stolen from my parents' home, which I had broken into to get some clothes and bandages that same early morning. I was so doped up on drugs and anger that I might have shot both Jimmy and his friend if I'd found them, but luckily I never saw either of them again.

Then, a few months before I was arrested by Officer Wright in December 1981, I had heard from a friend in the neighbourhood that Jimmy Brisbois had recently died from a drug overdose. By now it was nearly two years since Jimmy and his friend had almost killed me and I felt a kind of relief that I was no longer 'hunting him for revenge', but also that he could no longer come after me first for fear I was going to get even with him.

Now, sitting in my cell alone in the county jail following my arrest, I'd barely spoken to anyone. I'd tried to sleep as much as I could because it was the only way I could 'escape' from the whole situation and deal with my drug withdrawal. My whole body ached constantly and I was sick most of the time. My life seemed so hopeless that I considered suicide. I didn't even want my family to visit me, as I was too embarrassed to face them.

I don't know why, but as my idea of going forward to the police slowly developed I began to feel less doomed. In those first few days when I read and re-read the lone newspaper in my cell left by some other prisoner, I recalled that someone fairly reliable had told me that Jimmy had died of an overdose and that, after having stripped his body of anything worth taking, his friends had abandoned it in the Pine Barrens, a huge area of undeveloped woodlands in central New Jersey.

It was this which led me to think that if I told the police I had information implicating Jimmy in the rape and murder of Linda Mae Craig, then surely they would want to help me! Jimmy was dead, so they couldn't question him and ask for his alibi. If they went for it, I reasoned, they would see that I wasn't such a bad guy after all and hopefully they would give me credit for helping them solve such a horrific murder and then they'd go easy on me.

I played the story over and over in my head as I tried to build up my nerve. I knew the police would go over it in minute detail and try to catch me out in a lie if they could. So I had to get it straight in my own mind before I went to them. I also knew that I'd only have one chance at this, so it had to be right first time. When they became convinced I was telling them the truth, I reasoned, they'd let me out on bail and then I'd run as far away as I could.

My only concern was to get out of that prison any which way. Once I'd done that, the next stage was to get away from this madness. I rehearsed the story over and over until it sounded good – or at least to me it did.

It was time to tell the police.

First, I told Sergeant Gerald Murphy, the officer in charge of my housing block at the prison. After he heard me out on the initial details, he had me taken to the warden's office straight away to repeat it all. The warden, Thomas Rapone, listened to my story and, as he did so, he became more and more excited. He immediately phoned the detectives at the county prosecutor's office who had been working on the murder case. They were really surprised to hear from the warden of the local jail, but he told them he had significant information concerning the murder of Linda Mae Craig and they should come to his office as soon as possible to meet the man coming forward with the information.

He was so exuberant as he told the police these things that I have to admit, as I sat there listening to him, I too was caught up in the excitement of it all – even though I knew I had made up the entire story. Sergeant Murphy, whom I had originally gone to, was also in the warden's office. As I told the warden my story, I watched him from the corner of my eye as he kept glancing at me, like a proud father listening to his child impressing the teacher. I was no longer in solitary confinement worrying myself sick over attempted murder charges. Here I was sitting comfortably in the warden's office, sipping a cold drink and being told that I was a good person for coming forward with such valuable information about an unsolved murder. For the first time in a long while, I felt I was right back there in the normal world.

Detectives Clifton Minshall and David Pfeiffer soon arrived and introduced themselves to everyone. They said they couldn't understand how I had been charged so outlandishly with attempted murder and they intended to fix this situation if I showed that I could be of real help in solving such a big case. My ruse might actually have worked; it was all so unbelievably right how they were acting. I stopped being afraid that they would see through my lies and started to gain confidence in my shaky plans. I left the prison in the custody of the two detectives, and we headed to CID headquarters. There I met Detective Randy Martin, who was in charge of the unsolved murder case of Linda Mae Craig.

I explained that I knew a guy named Jimmy Brisbois and that we did things together, like steal cars to pay for our drugs, as we were both addicts. We'd steal the cars, then drive them from Philadelphia to the Delaware County area of Pennsylvania, south of the city, where we were not known. Then, one day in mid-December 1981, we'd been driving near the Tri-State shopping mall, just over the Pennsylvanian border into the state of Delaware.

It was while we were there in the parking lot that we'd decided to look for a certain type of car Jimmy said he could sell for a good price. I'd dropped Jimmy off at the mall for him to steal the car, and later we'd met up in Philadelphia, where he had paid me my share of the proceeds from the stolen car. And that was when he had told me what had happened in the mall parking lot.

I said that Jimmy had told me he'd seen a woman get into her car there and he'd abducted her after fighting with her for the keys, which she had refused to give him. Then he described how, having got her into the car, he'd raped and then murdered her. I told them I thought he was just drunk and boasting but that when I'd read about the murder in my prison cell, I'd quickly realised that the murder described in the newspaper was the same one Jimmy had been talking about.

It seemed to me that everyone in the room believed me. After thirty minutes or so, I was told I would be taken back to the jail from the prosecutor's office after making this formal statement. It all seemed so easy.

Once I'd finished my statement implicating Jimmy in the murder, I was even given a hot lunch and returned to jail with all sorts of assurances and promises of what would be done on my behalf with regard to the attempted murder charges. Detective Randy Martin, who was to be in charge of the investigation, had even called Benjamin Wright in front of me and had gotten the officer to admit that his charges were overblown and that if I provided real help in solving the murder he would reduce my charges to merely resisting arrest. I nearly cried as this was all explained to me.

When I arrived back in the Delaware County jail later that day, I was met by the warden, who again told me what a great job I'd done in cooperating with the detectives and helping to solve the murder. As a kind of 'early reward', he said, I would be placed in the general prison population rather than being put back into that nasty solitary confinement.

I was then taken from A-Block, where I had been kept on 22-hour lock-down, and placed in C-Block, where the men charged with more minor crimes were housed. I was allowed to walk around without any handcuffs and leg-irons on my hands and feet and I could mix freely with the other prisoners until my charges were resolved in the courts. This first gesture convinced me that I'd fooled them and my hopes of getting out were rising. I felt happier than I'd ever been since my arrest. I really thought my plan had worked and I truly believed that I was going to walk out of that prison soon.

Four days after I went to the police with my story about the murder, I was again taken to police headquarters. This time, however, when the detectives picked me up at the jail, there were no jovial greetings. It was all very business-like. Detective Martin was there with Detective Minshall and they were all silent and professional. I wondered what was going on, as nothing was really being said to me. Had they found Jimmy's body? Had they discovered that he was dead and I had played them for fools? I couldn't figure it out and nobody was talking to me. What the hell was happening?

As soon as we arrived at police headquarters, I found out what was what in short order. The police informed me that they'd found Jimmy Brisbois. He hadn't died of a drugs overdose as I'd been told. He was drug-free and holding down a job. What was more, he had an iron-clad alibi from his workplace for the time of the murder, so it was obvious that I had made up a lie about him.

I was stunned. I really had believed that Jimmy was dead. Now, as I sat there looking at the detectives, I became brutally aware that they knew my story about him and his involvement in this murder was a pack of lies. They stared at me, waiting to hear what I'd say next.

There was nothing else for me to do. I told them the truth. I said I was sorry for wasting their time, but I'd been desperate to get out of what seemed like a hopeless nightmare. I told them that I'd made the whole thing up because I couldn't face life in prison for something I hadn't done. Surely they could understand why I'd said what I'd said about this murder in view of what Detective Martin had told me about Officer Wright admitting that his charges had been overblown? Hadn't Officer Wright put the record straight and told them he'd embellished the whole incident? Surely they understood why I would make up such a story?

They listened to my pleading, then one of them said simply, 'Well, if Jimmy didn't carry out the murder, then *you* did.'

I couldn't believe what I'd just heard.

'How can you say that?' I blurted out. 'I don't know anything about this murder!'

I tried again to point out the false charges levelled at me by Officer Wright and how it was being accused of these serious felony counts which had driven me to create the lie to begin with.

The two detectives just stared at me unflinchingly across the interrogation room table. Then Detective Martin simply said in a calm voice, 'You know you did this murder and we know you did this murder. That's why you came to us, and now you're going to confess.'

I shook my head and stared back.

'You're crazy! I didn't commit this murder. I didn't kill anyone!' I yelled.

They just didn't want to hear it. I saw the look of contempt and hatred in Detective Martin's face. It was as if I'd personally insulted him by lying about Jimmy Brisbois and this murder case of which he was in charge.

'Yeah, well,' he went on coldly, 'you know the conversation that I told you that I had with Officer Wright about your charges? Well, guess what? Those charges are going to be prosecuted to the fullest now that you have lied to us. You'll be put away for life. The only chance you have of getting spared being strapped into the electric chair and executed for Mrs Craig's murder is to tell the truth about why you committed it.'

'Wait a minute. I didn't have anything to do with this murder,' I pleaded. 'I didn't kill anyone. This is all a mistake!'

But the police weren't interested in hearing that. For the next thirteen hours I was interrogated by these two detectives, who tried every trick they could to break me down into confessing to the crime. They did their utmost, short of beating the confession out of me, but I continued to deny any involvement. I even took a polygraph test and passed it, but that still didn't impress. All they kept saying over and over was: 'We know you killed her. We know you did it.' Then, in an effort to try and make me lose control one last time, Detective Martin started taunting me: 'You know I spoke to your girlfriend Teresa and she and I had a long talk.'

There was glee in his voice.

What are you talking about? I thought. *What does Terri have to do with anything?*

'We know you split up with her and it drove you crazy and that's why you did this murder. You got all twisted up over her leaving you for some other guy she was sleeping with and you snapped.'

Then they explained how they thought that in my mental anguish I had gone out looking for a girl to kill who looked like her – who turned out to be Linda Mae Craig – and that I'd raped her and ended up by stabbing her to death.

I simply couldn't believe what I was hearing. As I listened to them telling me this ridiculous story I just kept thinking: *You must both be insane! How can you make up this crazy theory about my ex-girlfriend and try and use it to make it look as if I had a reason to kill Mrs Craig?*

On and on they went. They tried every way they could to get me to admit that I was the killer, yet I refused to admit to something I knew nothing about. At one point during the interrogation Detective Martin even boasted how he'd had sex with Terri, hoping that it would provoke a response.

It worked, because I blew up at them. I made no damning confession, but I shouted stupid things about what I should have done to Terri and they twisted it all around. I soon realised that these people would never believe that I'd had nothing to do with this murder and that any words that came out of my mouth were going to be twisted around to make it seem like I did it.

Eventually I told them that enough was enough. I wasn't saying another word. I didn't care what they said or did to me. I wasn't playing their game any longer.

They took me back to the prison that night and, as I rode along in the back of that police car sinking deeper and deeper into my own misery, I knew that I was doomed.

As a punishment for 'playing the prison staff for fools', as the warden put it, I was immediately taken back to A-Block again and placed in a solitary confinement cell. The one they stuck me in had three panes missing from its window glass, which were letting in the freezing January air.

As I sat there in the biting cold, I realised that my lies had just made everything so much more of a nightmare for me. I was at an all-time low and I had no idea how to get out of it. Surely things couldn't get any worse?

4 The blackest pit

A few days after I had been sent back into solitary confinement on A-Block, I was lying on my bed just drifting through endless thoughts of my world being crushed, when suddenly, without any warning, a bucket of filthy mop water was thrown over me, and three inmates let out of their cells for exercise attacked me through the cell bars. When I leapt to my feet in response, one of them threw powdered scouring bleach at my eyes while another tried to poke me in the face with a broom handle sharpened into a spear. The third was the one who had thrown the mop water over me. At first I didn't understand what it was all about.

'You're all nuts!' I screamed. 'You're crazy! What's this shit all about?'

'You're a fucking snitch!' they shouted. 'We know you are a police informant and that you're trying to rat on someone over a murder to get out of prison!'

'You're gonna die, you fuckin' rat!' one of them yelled as he tossed urine from a plastic jar into my face through the bars.

I tried to grab my mattress and barricade my door to defend myself.

All the while, the guard on duty in the cell block acted as if he were telling them to stop what they were doing while standing safely inside his office thirty yards away. He couldn't care less what happened to me; the only thing he cared about was that he didn't have to do all the paperwork that would be generated if they succeeded in hurting me seriously.

I realised that the world around me had just turned to complete shit, and I was scared. These inmates were all members of a motorcycle gang that had a history of murder and violence. In prison, a 'snitch' is considered one of the lowest forms of life. Right down at the bottom, along with child molesters, corrupt police officers and rapists.

I was to learn months later that, on the day prior to this first attack, the leader of the motorcycle gang had been transported to the prison from court. Some police officers were discussing my case in front of this gang member, knowing that details of my trying to implicate Jimmy Brisbois in the murder of Mrs Craig would filter back into the prison. The officers must have known that the gang members would torment me and expose me as an informant and that I'd be attacked by other prisoners as well. They no doubt hoped this added stress would push me into telling them what they wanted to hear.

This little ruse almost cost me my life at the hands of men made miserable by their own lives. For these inmates saw hurting me as a way of venting all their own anger. I was a symbol of every reason why they were there and I was going to pay for it.

During the week that followed that first attack, it seemed as if everyone on the cell block had declared war on Nick Yarris. I had urine, bleach and worse thrown all over me again as I sat huddled on my bed. I was constantly threatened and called a 'rat'. The other prisoners beat me up if I came out of my cell to shower off the filth they had thrown on me. The gang also kept telling me how I was going to die as soon as they got to me when there were no witnesses around. At the time I didn't realise that I had been set up. All I knew was that somehow they knew what I had tried to do to Jimmy Brisbois and they were determined to get me for it.

I quickly decided that I had little left to lose. The guards were not going to be able to stop every attack and I had had enough of the constant abuse. I simply went to war. From then on, every time my cell door was opened, I went out fighting. Early on, it seemed as if the fighting might never end. I got hurt trying to punch two or even three guys at once. Yet I also hurt some of my tormentors enough for them to see that I didn't care how many of them I took on and I feared no one.

But after only a week of fighting off every guy who wanted a piece of me, I could take no more. One night, the haunting thoughts in my head just got the better of me and I gave up. I wrapped a sheet around my neck and hanged myself from the radiator mounted to the top of my cell wall. I was hanging there when a guard found me after a few minutes and cut me down. The guard later told me that he thought I was a sick-minded person who had actually done the murder but that he wanted me to live only so that I could suffer more by being in prison for the rest of my days.

I was twenty years old and this was my first attempt at taking my own life. I had been reckless and wild in the past, but never before had I made a serious effort to kill myself outright. I felt like something inside me was dead, that I really had stopped caring. When I was cut down from my homemade noose, the guards took me to the hospital, where I was put into four-point restraints and placed on suicide watch.

A few days later, Sergeant Murphy came to see me there in the hospital wing. Although he only talked to me briefly, there was something about the way he spoke that made me believe he really cared about me. I was so miserable that I just lay there shackled to the bed, crying for hours. At that time I had no friends, no one I could talk to. My family still hadn't visited or made contact.

All I could think about was that I might be spending the rest of my life in prison and there was no help coming. I wanted to believe there was someone who cared, but I kept seeing everyone there as just another user or liar.

Sergeant Murphy arranged for me to be transferred back to A-Block, where he swore he would have me placed in protection and separated from the other inmates during the time I was allowed out of my cell. He told me that he would personally get rid of any officer who let inmates throw things on me. Despite his assurances, though, I knew that he was powerless to do a whole lot for me. But I didn't care. I didn't give a damn about anything at that point. I was just empty inside.

As soon as I was placed back on A-Block the verbal abuse began again, although I did my best to ignore it. After my return from the hospital they had put me in what is called a 'strip-cell'; that is, a cell with no sheets or towel and no clothing that could be used for a noose. I was allowed only a very thick, coarse 'horse blanket' to protect me from the freezing cold. As I lay there naked on my plastic mattress, inmates walked by during their exercise time, mocking me and taunting me.

After four days of this I requested to see Sergeant Murphy and asked him for my belongings back. I wanted my transistor radio, my sheets and some clothing so that I could deal with the cold and have something to listen to that would drown out the noise of all the inmates nearby.

He looked at me for a long moment. 'Nick, are you telling the police the truth?' he began. 'Look, I can get your stuff back but you've got to promise me not to kill yourself. You've also got to tell the truth about this murder because you must get this off your chest.' He appeared genuinely concerned.

At this I broke down. I simply couldn't take it any more and I began to weep.

Murphy began gently: 'Why don't you just tell me what happened? Then I can go to the police and help you,' he said.

This time I thought that maybe if I just told him I knew who had committed the murder and I had been involved somehow to a lesser degree, but more than what I'd said earlier to police, he might just be able to help me. I knew it was going to be another lie, but what choice did I have? In my misery, I felt I had none.

'Well, hypothetically,' I said, 'what if I participated in the crime but I didn't actually do the murder? Would that help?'

'Absolutely!' he replied. 'That's what we could use. We could go to the police with that.'

'Listen,' I said. 'Maybe if I said I did the rape but didn't do the murder. Is that good enough?'

'That's excellent!' he went on. 'We can bargain with that.'

I broke down again.

'OK, if that's what you want, I'll tell them that.'

He immediately called the warden to tell him what he had just gotten out of me and to ask him to call the detectives again so I could be picked up and taken back to their offices.

During the ride to the prosecutors' office, I suddenly realised the craziness of my situation and decided once and for all to tell the truth.

'Look,' I told the detectives when I got there, 'this has gone too far. I know nothing about the murder. I didn't have anything to do with it.'

I tried to tell them that I was going crazy in the cell with the cold and the noise from being teased and I just wanted my radio and my clothes back. But they would have none of it.

'You've confessed to Sergeant Murphy,' they said. 'That's good enough reason to have you arrested right now.'

'This is insane!' I replied, but no one wanted to believe anything I said now. After what seemed like endless hours of interrogation, during which I still made no confession, they angrily took me back to prison.

I had no idea what they were going to do. Everything was all twisted and bent and I was lost mentally. I lay there that night just exhausted, listening to the men nearby taunt and tease me for having been taken out of the prison and returned so late. They were convinced I had been out with the police pinning crimes on others, for which they were promising me all sorts of reprisals.

The next morning I was awoken early by the guards, who told me I was going to court. When I explained that I was not due for any court hearing, they ignored me and dragged me out of my cell to the prison entrance. Here I was met by a smiling Detective Martin, who cheerfully announced that he was there to take me before a local judge to have me charged with the kidnapping, rape and murder of Linda Mae Craig. It was 2 February 1982.

I never even said a word during the entire ride down to the courthouse. I just sat with my face pressed against the glass of the car window and wept in utter despair. With me were two policemen. One was an officer from Trainer, Pennsylvania, as the murder of Mrs Craig had happened over the county border in his precinct. The other was the lead detective in the Delaware County homicide division, Randy Martin. He kept taunting me as we drove along, for the amusement of this other officer.

When the judge read my charges in the courtroom, he kept asking me if I understood them and that each charge carried a punishment of life imprisonment or a possible death sentence. Since they were such serious charges, there was no chance of bail. I could not even bring my eyes up to look at him.

After the brief hearing, I numbly went back to jail and collapsed on my bed, oblivious to all the shouts of the men who thought I was out testifying against others. I just lay there, not even bothering to block my cell door with my mattress, as I'd done before when men threw things on me. I didn't even move when they threw mop water at me as they passed by. I thought that this was going to be my day-to-day existence for ever. That I had been consigned to a hell of my own making and nothing was going to save me. I just went blank inside.

Somewhere in each of us is the blackest pit from which few ever return. I had found mine, lying there that day in the urine and filthy mop water that had been tossed on me like I was a human sewer.

It took a few days for the inmates to begin leaving me alone. Once the newspapers came out and the local television and radio broadcast the news that I alone had been charged with the rape and murder of Mrs Craig, they realised that I couldn't have been an informant as there was no co-defendant involved. Now they just saw me as some mental deviant who had gone out and stalked an innocent woman because she looked like my ex-girlfriend. So, although I felt temporarily better because I was no longer being viciously attacked, my spirits were not lifted for long.

What really began to pull me down was how the prison staff treated me. It stole all my self-confidence to be treated as if I were psychotic. It was so demeaning when the guards or nurses or counsellors all talked to me as if I were a true deviant. I could hardly stand it. I stopped communicating and just sank deep into myself.

What happened next was all part of the homicide detectives' attempt to seal their case against me. They had the prison staff place a man called Charles Catalino in the cell next to mine. I had already been charged with the rape and murder of Mrs Craig based on the statements I was alleged to have made to both prison guards and police.

But the police were up against a huge problem: Mrs Craig had last been seen at the shopping mall at 4.05 p.m. on 15 December 1981 – and a co-worker of Mrs Craig claimed that she had seen me at the mall. But four people – my mother, my father, my sister Sissy as well as a local shop-keeper from whom I had bought a cold drink and some chewing gum – were prepared to testify that I had been at or near my home between 4.30 and 4.45 p.m. on the after-noon of the murder.

That made it near impossible for me to have committed the crime and then driven the twenty-plus miles (in December rush-hour traffic, no less) from the murder scene back to my house within the given time frame.

Now, when this Catalino guy moved into the cell next to mine it seemed no big deal. Cell moves in small county jails like Delaware County's are common as prisoners are either released or make bail. In fact, before he moved, Catalino had been stopping by my cell door for a few days talking to me and saying how messed up it was that I had been charged with rape and murder and he thought I was being framed.

He said he knew all about William Ryan, the district attorney assigned to prosecute me, as the reason he was in jail was that he had burgled this man's home. I did not believe him initially, but Charles showed me the news clip-pings about his case and he laughed at how he'd degraded the prosecutor's home. Apparently, he faced ten to twenty years in prison for this, in addition to the four to ten years he was serving for other burglaries. Charles claimed, with near glee, that he was the prisoner most hated by the local authorities as he had stolen all sorts of secret documents from the prosecutor's home. He even tried to imply that there was a bounty on his head. I just took his talk as what guys in prison do to impress others.

In his mid-thirties, Charles was a heroin addict who even had needle marks on his neck as he had burned out his arms from so many years of drug abuse. Tall and lanky, he had once been good-looking, but years of taking drugs had ravaged his face and made it look real gaunt. He was the first prisoner to file a lawsuit against Delaware County for not having any sort of methadone treatment for heroin addicts.

But Charles Catalino also had a plan, which I never saw coming, what with everything else that was going on. This man saw me as *his* possible way out of an endless jail sentence, just as I had done with Jimmy Brisbois. He had watched from afar as all the drama around me had unfolded. And then he had come up with a plan to inveigle his way into my confidence by showing me his 'credentials' and making himself out to be as hated as me. All the while he and his girlfriend were coordinating a deal with detectives that in return for his freedom he would befriend me and get me to confess that my concrete alibi was a lie. That was all they needed him to do and then the case against me was a slam dunk, the prosecution felt. By the time I found out about the deal between the detectives and Charles, I was already in a new cell inside the Chester County jail.

Although there were continued tensions between me and some of the other prisoners in Delaware County jail, I had no clue why I had been transferred. I had not been accused of any crimes in Chester County, so I had not been put there to face criminal charges. I knew something was wrong; I just had no idea what it was. One morning in April 1982 I was simply told to gather up my stuff as I was being moved. It was that quick. Once in Chester County jail, not only was I put in solitary confinement because of the seriousness of the charges against me, but the new jail staff treated me as if I were mentally deranged and so violent that Delaware County could not deal with me. Only a few staff knew the real reason that I had been sent there: that Charles Catalino was cooperating with detectives and they wanted to keep me apart from him. I had no idea my old cell was being photographed as the location of my so-called confession to Charles, made, he claimed, when he had been standing at the next-door cell window. He also claimed that I had confessed to him that I was afraid that my alibi witnesses would be caught in a lie and that, further, I was sure they had found my blood on the victim.

I learned about this 'confession' when a sheaf of documents was passed to my defence attorney as they began swearing in the jury at my trial for the attempted murder and kidnapping of Officer Benjamin Wright. I remember the prosecutor, a man named Barry Gross, handing them over boldly to my lawyer and adding: 'Read it and weep, counsellor!'

Having read it, my trial attorney, Sam Stretton, turned to me and asked who the hell this Charles Michael Catalino was. Then he added: 'How come the police have these statements from him in which he claims you made all these admissions about the murder case?'

I sat there, my head spinning and the blood drained from my face as I read Charles's detailed account of how I had told him that I had gotten my mother and father and sister all to lie about where I'd been on the night of the murder.

Up until that moment, at least I had been able to defend myself to others by pointing out that four people had all given me an alibi. But suddenly I could feel my will to defend myself dissolve inside of me.

My mind raced through each time this man had come by my cell and all the many different reasons he had given for doing so. I realised my initial instincts about him had been right, but he had duped me into overriding them with his deceptively passive manner.

When the courtroom was called to order for proceedings to start against me I just sat glued to my seat, my eyes devouring each page of the statements. I felt hands yanking me up out of my chair as the judge ordered me to stand. Two deputy sheriffs had grabbed me by either arm when His Honour had become annoyed at my lack of respect in not standing with everyone else when he came into the courtroom. As he banged on his podium with his gavel he glared at me for my defiant act. I do not even recall much of what he said as my head was just swimming with all sorts of thoughts.

This was getting really terrifying. The police were prepared to let a junkie who had been the most hated man in jail go free just for saying that I was worried my family would be found out as liars at my murder trial. And if they were willing to let this man go free for just one lie, then how far were they willing to go to get a conviction?

5 Round One in the contest for my life

Before being tried for the rape and murder of Linda Mae Craig, I first had to face trial in Delaware County, Pennsylvania, for the attempted kidnapping and murder of Officer Benjamin Wright – all of which gave the local press a lot of material to play with. They simply accepted the claims of the police about both crimes and filled their pages theorising about my possible motives.

The trial was set for late April 1982 before Judge Robert F. Kelly. As the court process rolled over me, no matter how angry I felt towards others and what they were doing to me, I knew that in truth I had put myself here. This thought was always haunting me, always undercutting any courage I could muster. I was shamed by my own actions into not making a fuss as I placed all my belief in my attorney, Sam Stretton, to help me through this.

The evidence for the attempted kidnapping and murder of Officer Wright essentially boiled down to two different versions of the same event as recounted by the only two people who were there: one, a respected local police officer;

44

the other, a 20-year-old drug addict and car thief. No one expected the trial to last long and there was little doubt about its outcome.

The trial began with Officer Wright taking the witness stand to tell his version. He had, he said, been parked in his patrol car alongside an elevated section of road above the part of Interstate I-95 that cut through the city of Chester, Pennsylvania, where his patrol section was, at 1.45 a.m. when he noticed a bright orange 1970s Chevrolet Camaro with wide rear tyres fail to stop properly at a stop sign. He therefore pulled out of his parked position in order to initiate a traffic stop on this car.

Once the orange Camaro stopped alongside the overpass to I-95, the driver exited the car and then, without provocation, simply attacked Officer Wright. After having punched him twice, knocking his eyeglasses from his face, the driver took his gun. Officer Wright then testified how he had tried to overpower the Camaro driver but the driver attempted to force him into the car and abduct him, having struck him with the pistol across his face while doing so. The officer therefore decided to lunge for the weapon, grabbing the man's arm, thereby managing to wrestle control of the gun from his attacker, but not before the gun went off inches from his face.

I had heard the officer's version of events twice before this point, and it angered me how he embellished it more and more each time – but also how he seemed to show real open hatred towards me while doing it. In court I just sat there in my thick plastic jailhouse glasses wanting to cry.

I was unable to look at this man as he testified, as I could never forget that I was a junkie, a car thief and a loser. It didn't matter that I knew he was lying, it just crushed me that I was now sitting there with my family listening to how I was such a waste. Yet the trial was not about what I felt like, it was about twelve jurors who were there to ensure it was fair. And they could see as well as anyone else in the court that day the open hostility this man kept beaming out towards me, mindless of how it looked to others. I just kept my head down, weighed down by so many stones under which my soul seemed to be buried.

Next it was my attorney's turn to ask the witness questions. How many times had I struck him with my fists, and how many with his own gun? The officer replied that I had punched him twice and then hit him in the face twice with his gun, a model no. 10 Smith & Wesson .38 pistol. My attorney asked the officer to review the lone photograph of his injuries, which showed a 2-cm scratch on his right hand between the thumb and forefinger, where he said his gun had been taken from him. This photograph was his sole proof of the violence that had apparently taken place. Why, asked my trial attorney, did he not photograph his face? Having had his eyeglasses punched off of his face and having been pistol-whipped; surely there were marks there as well?

After a long beat, the officer quipped, 'I heal fast. And besides, I'm a good-looking man, I don't want anyone to see my face all bruised up.'

Many people in the courtroom, including some of the jury, made noises of disbelief at this answer. I think everyone knew at this point that the officer's story was untrue. Now it was up to me to tell my version and hope that justice would win out. My story was simple. I was driving home from a nightclub, it was late and I had gotten a bit twisted about on the roads going by Interstate I-95.

I was trying to locate the road, which allowed you to access I-95 North, when I saw flashing lights come on behind me. This made me panic-stricken and fearful because of the beating I had taken for running from the police in early December 1981 – and I showed the jury photos of my face from that first beating.

I tried to explain how I literally froze with fear. I even got down from the stand and, with the help of my lawyer, acted out my version of events, showing how the only scratch the officer got was from when he reached for his gun and I panicked and grabbed his arm before the gun went off.

The jury did not take long to come to their decision. Less than an hour.

The reaction in the courtroom was unexpected. As the verdicts of 'Not guilty' rang out, the room exploded into angry shouting, mostly from Officer Wright, outraged that a jury had taken the word of a junkie and a thief over his. Judge Kelly let it all go as he thanked the jury and walked out in disgust. Then there was another outburst, this time from the district prosecutor, Barry Gross. As he walked towards the exit, past where I was sitting at the defence table, he turned abruptly and hissed in my face, 'You will *never* leave this county alive, do you hear me!'

In his view his career had just taken a huge hit, as I had raped and murdered Mrs Craig and for that he hated me to the core. As I stared into his eyes it dawned on me that I need not be so ashamed any more. A jury had just lifted a huge stone from off my grave, and I could feel my spirit begin to come back. I looked him right in the face and kept my head up. I was no longer going to cower before these people.

I had never even laid eyes on Mrs Craig and now I was going to fight for myself because in my next trial it was not just my word against that of a police officer. I suddenly felt blessed as I looked across the courtroom at my mother and father: my family knew exactly where I had been at the time of Mrs Craig's death. I looked at Barry Gross and smiled.

My refusal to bow in the face of such hatred pushed the prosecutor over the edge. He took the folder containing the case file and threw it against the wall just by the exit door. Then he stormed out into the lobby and accosted the jury, telling them they had 'let a murderer go!' At which point a female juror bravely pointed out to him that they weren't there to try me for murder, they had only heard *this* case in which the prosecution witness had clearly lied.

It was my shaken mother who witnessed this exchange, but when she asked my trial attorney if this was something we could use to show that the prosecution case was becoming a personal attack on me, he told her simply, 'Unfortunately, as the parent of the accused, you have no credibility. You are as much a suspect on trial as your son, so any evidence based on actions by the prosecutor you say you have witnessed will be worthless.'

Every time she would come to visit me in prison and retell this story – which she must have done a hundred times – I would look into my mother's eyes knowing that the greatest hurt to her in all this was that she and the rest of my family were suffering just for being my family. She too was being put on trial for bearing a child who had been accused of such heinous crimes. I think this is one of the toughest aspects of the trial process: what it does to everyone around the accused. It was exhausting me, but on the other hand I did not care if they hired twenty inmates to claim I had confessed to this crime. I was going to stand up for myself in my next trial. I was not going to sit through it passively and let my family watch me be broken by it all. Sadly, I was going to need every bit of my newly renewed strength and willpower in the days that followed my acquittal.

I was soon to learn exactly what the prosecutor meant when he spat that threat in my face about how I was not going to leave the county alive. One week after the trial for the attempted murder of Benjamin Wright I learned that that same prosecutor had asked to take over the prosecution for the murder of Linda Mae Craig. Further, that *he* was now seeking the death penalty.

In the months that followed my arrest for the rape and murder of Mrs Craig, not a single factor about that crime had changed, except for one. I was found *not guilty* in a trial conducted by this particular prosecutor. For him now to seek the death penalty when the record throughout the earlier court proceedings all stated that a general charge of second degree murder (which carried a life sentence) was being sought, was, in my view nothing less than vengeance.

Why was it such a big deal that I be put to death now? The facts of the crime were that Mrs Craig had been abducted in the state of Delaware, as evidenced by her shoes being found in the mall parking lot near to where her car had been parked. However, her body had been found later in the state of Pennsylvania. But no one had witnessed where the crimes of rape and murder had actually occurred. Legally, therefore, only a court in Pennsylvania could hold a trial for the charge of murder, whereas the charges of rape and kidnapping had to be tried in the state in which they had been committed.

By law, any fair hearing in Pennsylvania was going to have to rule that the murder charges could not proceed as a capital case because legally they could not take into account possible exacerbating crimes, which had been committed outside the Pennsylvanian court's jurisdiction.

That was when I learned that not only was I going to face the same prosecutor as in my first trial, but also the same trial judge.

It looked like both had chosen to take on this prosecution in an effort to right the perceived wrong they each felt had been dealt earlier. Nor did the prosecutor bother to hide his feelings about me – he went to the press with interviews and comments as well.

And Judge Robert Kelly's first act when he took over the trial for the murder of Mrs Craig was to allow the prosecutor to seek the death penalty. He further ruled that it was not necessary for a jury to decide the exact location and jurisdiction of the lesser crimes of rape and kidnapping as 'aggravating circumstances' in order for a capital trial to take place. I do not know how else to put it, but in my view this was nothing less than attempted murder by a public official, using his power in order to try and ensure that I was killed.

My attorney, Sam Stretton, weakly fought this attempt as an outright abuse of the law. And for the prosecutor to seek the death penalty only one month before trial and then withhold crucial witness statements pointing towards other suspects was no less an attempted murder than had this man simply pulled out a gun and shot me in court that day he had threatened me.

The real surprise was how the media seemed to be in concert with the prosecutor. Not once questioning why the county prosecutor was seeking my death having just lost another case against me, the press began to spew forth stories about how I had stalked the victim prior to the murder because she bore a fatal resemblance to my former girlfriend.

A fair trial was out of the question.

6 Commonwealth vs Nicholas James Yarris

Until this point, I had been willing to fight for myself, with my family standing behind me all the way, but boy, was I up against it now. Even I could see that this second trial was not going to be the cordial, polite affair I had hoped for, conducted in accordance with the law. Everything about this trial was going to be different from the first one. No mistakes, no mess-ups. They were going to get a conviction.

The battle for my life began on Tuesday 29 June 1982. And from his opening address it was clear that His Honour Justice Robert Kelly was not here to conduct a lengthy trial with fairness at its core. As he talked to the jury assembled in their jury box, he pointed out how he shared their obvious worries that they might miss out on the forthcoming holiday celebrations due to their obligations as jurors. He assured them, however, that they need not be concerned. Although it was Tuesday afternoon and this was a capital murder trial, he intended to have it wrapped up by Friday so that they could all go home and celebrate the Fourth of July.

My jaw dropped open when I heard this. How could a judge preside fairly over a trial in which the defendant stood condemned to death if his main concern appeared to be to make sure that it was all over in time for everyone to get home for hotdogs and fireworks? Fuming inside, I willed Judge Kelly to look at me, but he did not.

I kept my head up throughout the whole trial. I watched as a parade of people took the stand and openly lied about what I was supposed to have said or done. I was sickened as Charles Catalino came to the stand wearing a dress shirt with the collar turned up like some bad Elvis impersonator in order to hide the needle tracks on his neck. We were not allowed to bring up his many years of heroin addiction in our defence, yet my own drug use was stated throughout the trial.

It was numbing to watch as a female co-worker of the victim took the witness stand to claim that she had seen me at the mall numerous times – including in the days *after* the crime, when she testified that I came back and asked her if she knew that the victim had been raped. She said she was shocked I had said this, as at the time she had not even known this to be true.

A detective produced what he alleged were notes he had made to himself on a microcassette *after* the thirteen-hour interrogation on 27 January 1982 in which I was supposed to have made my damning admissions of guilt. He claimed that he had had this tape of 'powerful evidence' transcribed later by a secretary. But he lied. He simply lied. And I just stared at the side of his face as he did so.

In Pennsylvania, recording an interrogation without the subject's permission is a felony, which, as a violation of the wiretap laws, can carry up to a ten-year prison sentence – and the detective knew that. Which was why he claimed he had made the notes after the interrogation. However, what he failed to take into account was that the stenographer he asked to transcribe the tape was trained to write down every single noise in the background to a conversation, not just the conversation itself, so if she was transcribing notes made by the detective after the event there would only have been his voice.

However, the transcript of my so-called 'confession' also included descriptions of background noises such as 'quiet sob' or 'nervous laugh', underlined and in brackets. Things like: 'I [sob] never meant to kill anyone. I need help'; or 'I [cough] think I have said too much.' It was obvious. Why on earth could no one else see that this was all a huge lie?

As much as I tried desperately to get everyone to listen to me, they paid no attention, let alone understood the implications of what I was saying. It felt as if my mouth was full of mush, as the more I pointed out that this *proved* he was lying, the less anyone heard me.

And then the biggest bomb of all was dropped. It came so subtly and so unexpectedly. The deceased's husband was called to the witness stand, and during his testimony he was asked to view a series of photos projected to the whole courtroom on an eight-foot-square screen. At first he was shown simple family photographs of his wife with himself and their children. An emotional charge entered the court-room and I had no way to deal with both the shame and empathy that I felt for this man. I tried not to look, but I too was drawn by the images on the screen. Then there followed horrific photographs of the interior of the victim's car, cov-ered in blood. But it was one particular image that truly changed everything for me at this trial.

It was a black and white photograph of the snow-covered parking lot in which Mrs Craig's body had been discovered the morning after her murder. It was an overview taken from an elevated height so that you could see the entire area surrounding her body as it lay there half-hidden in the snow. In the photograph two sets of footprints could be seen clearly.

They began as simple, side-by-side prints approaching the spot where the body lay, but suddenly they became erratic and scattered and blood-filled. These were the prints of the two children who had found Mrs Craig's body and then fled as soon as they realised what it was. The photo-graph had a stillness and an eeriness that perfectly captured the desolation of the scene. And it was that combination of innocence and gore that gave it its power. You could even see where one child had walked over and kicked the body, thinking it was a mannequin lying there.

I swear, that jury took one long look at me after having seen that photo and it was the last time they ever looked at me again. That was the exact moment in my trial when my conviction was sealed. It wasn't the lies or the falsifications by witnesses; it was the jury's reaction to that one photo. I too felt it in every fibre of my body: the true horror of her death.

So there I was, all of twenty-one years of age, my chin jutting out, not even sure whether I should be proud or angry. I thought I was going to be able to face the next part of the trial with equanimity, not least because I simply had not committed the crime.

On Thursday mid-afternoon, 1 July 1982, the jury was given the case to deliberate. As promised by Judge Kelly on the Tuesday, they would be given this case to decide after just a couple of days. They were left to review the evidence and testimonies presented by each side, along with the fact that I was B+ blood type (only nine per cent of the US population share this blood group) – the same as that of the sperm found on the victim's clothing.

The prosecutor urged the jury to think of all the alleged statements made out of my own mouth, while the defence attorney pointed to my alibi and how many people would have had to conspire to lie on my behalf.

The jury went out to a local restaurant to have dinner and decide my fate. Again, His Honour wanted them to be inconvenienced as little as possible, so he had allowed them to eat as they deliberated and not be caught up in the holiday traffic before leaving for the weekend.

Meanwhile I sat in my cell located directly behind the courtroom on the second floor of the courthouse. I had been sent there each day before and after the proceedings in court while the jury was being seated. In summer it was a real nice place to sit: while being secluded from the other prisoners I was able to look out over the courtyard below. I could watch the women and children walking by and it almost gave me the feeling that I was once again back in civilisation. I could almost touch the little scenes unfolding outside. I often found myself just drinking in every nuance of the actions of the passers-by, the way they spoke, the way they walked.

But that day, as I sat there with my face pressed against the mesh screen over the slightly raised window, I just breathed in the rain-scented air. Storm clouds were gathering and any moment now it was going to pelt down and pelt down all weekend, thwarting any party plans those jurors might have.

Then, as if on cue, the skies opened and lightning struck. The suddenness of the storm was so powerful and its timing so perfect that it was as if my prayers had been answered and I was lifted for a moment. A few minutes later there was a power cut and this eerie yellow emergency lighting flickered on throughout the courthouse building.

The sheriff's deputies came and stood by the bars to my cell, making jokes about how God was having his say about the weekend fireworks. This was their attempt at a kind gesture – they had no axe to grind with me, they were simply doing their job.

They had seen what effect the trial was having on my family and they knew that I was just about to face a very tough moment, which very few people have to confront in their lives. I had no problems with the deputies and they showed me no ill treatment throughout my ordeal; in fact, I was actually glad they had come to take away my lonesome thoughts.

We stood for a few moments on either side of my cell door not really saying anything, then, again as if on cue, the storms let up a bit and, just like that, the Clerk of the Courts appeared in the hallway to alert us that the jury was back from the restaurant and had reached their verdict.

One of the deputies said in a mocking way, 'Gee, I hope they left room for dessert for them to enjoy during the penalty phase.' (In the United States, unlike in Britain, it is the jury, not the judge, that usually decides the penalty as well as the verdict.) The comment was not meant to be funny and no one laughed. Even the deputies felt bad about how my trial had been conducted.

Back inside the courtroom, I sat down willing myself not to cry, just biting the hell out of the inside of my mouth as I watched each jury member pass by me. Not one had the nerve to look at me. As the last one passed, I knew that I was going to be found guilty. I stilled my breathing and looked hard at the side of the judge's face as he spoke to the jury. Then I was asked to stand up and face them alone. My knees shook. I waited.

After being asked the verdict, the jury foreman read aloud: 'Guilty of the charge of murder in the first degree.' Silence. Then, after a pause, the jury foreman announced the next verdict: 'Guilty of rape.'

It was at this moment that my sister Mabel, sitting two rows behind me, made this strange guttural noise. I have heard many agonised sounds of human beings in suffering in my life, but I have never heard such a pitiful sound as this, before or since. It was as if she were being ripped to shreds by the sheer weight of the thought that her brother was a rapist/murderer. She knew what they did in prison to men convicted of such crimes. She knew that they were going to torment me, and as a convicted sex offender I would be a target for anyone and everyone. She knew I had already been abused and assaulted, but what the future held was even worse.

I turned around and called her by her family nickname, saying only, 'Sissy, please!' as I could not bear to hear her agony. But she could not look at me and then I too finally broke down in tears. I turned and looked at the jury, many of whom were also crying. I even found it in myself to feel pity for them, too. They had been used and lied to in no less a fashion than the many other people in that courtroom.

But I should have saved my pity for those who needed it more. As I was to find out later from that same deputy who had made the joke about the jury saving their desserts till the penalty phase, in fact several of the jurors had indeed placed their dessert orders with the waiters during their main meal order so that their treats would be ready for them to eat as they decided whether I should live or die. As the deputy described it to me, I could really picture the scene as the jury tried to hurry their dessert order along.

How they could sit there and enjoy such delicious treats as they decided the fate of a 21-year-old man was beyond me. Thank God that, unlike them, I do not have to live with that on my conscience.

As we waited for the penalty to be delivered, I was once more returned to my cell above the courtyard. What I saw next I will never forget. People were pouring out of the courtroom doors, many of them celebrating and shouting their congratulations to the victors in my prosecution, who were just standing there lighting cigarettes and laughing or grouped by the doorway in the early evening sunlight. I saw the faces of my neighbours who had attended the trial over the past three days as they joked and made sounds of human flesh cooking in the electric chair. I saw people whom I had known as a boy, whose children I had hung around with, people who had allowed me to eat in their homes, stand there and laugh about me. Then some of them spotted me watching from above and they began to gesture up at me. They knew I was never coming back, regardless of what the jury decided, as I faced a minimum of life in prison. So they started jeering at me. I had my hands cuffed behind my back, so I could not make any gestures at them, but I faced them and sneered back while I carved every moment into my memory.

Being sentenced to death by the jury came as no shock to me. I did not even flinch when they read out the verdict. I just stood there staring right at the judge, waiting for every time he nearly made eye contact with me, willing him to look into my face. My parents and a few members of the victim's family were virtually the only people left in the courtroom by then. Even the jeerers did not come back, as they needed to get going for the all-important holiday weekend.

Once the jury finished the sentence portion of the trial, I turned and looked at my family huddled in the seats behind me. They were hugging each other. The jury's recommendation that I be put to death had crumpled them.

Most people were getting up to leave by now and I was just about to be led back to my cell. But I desperately wanted to say goodbye to my family before I went, so I resisted the pull on my arms and kept saying 'Mom' over and over again in a mid-level voice as I willed her to look up at me. I couldn't see her face as she was cradling it in my father's arms. Then I heard a loving voice say, 'Just go, Nicky.' And only then, when I heard those words, did I give in and allow myself to be led away without saying my final farewell.

As I left I turned my head round and watched in agony as my family was left there clutching each other in full public view, having seen one of their own be condemned to be executed. This time the deputies took me to a cell under the courthouse used for regular prisoners as they gathered up the gear needed to put me in the car. They had been told to get me out of there and back to jail fast. However, they allowed my trial attorney to come and see me briefly before I left. As soon as I met his eyes we both began to weep. I felt so defeated, yet it was I who reached out to comfort him and ease his pain, stroking his shoulder through the metal bars of my cell. He told me how he would save me from this fate no matter what.

I didn't have the energy to believe in hope right then, so I simply lowered my eyes at his eager attempts to get me to trust him one more time. I had been dealt so many blows by the system by then that I almost expected to be cheated by it. The very reason this man had become a defence attorney was his belief that the law was fair and that justice would be done. Now his whole career had been undermined and his belief in the fairness of the due process of law shown to be useless in the face of those who would bend it to their own personal will.

7 Sometimes the road leads to dark places

I was sent to Death Row at the age of twenty-one, the second youngest of the twenty-seven men sentenced to die in Pennsylvania in 1982. Imagine what it is like to know that you are not just going to prison, but that you are going to be put to death at some time in the future – although you don't know when.

America currently has nearly 3,500 men and women waiting to die in prisons across the country. While they vary in their individual settings, nearly all face a similar situation to the one I faced back in 1982. A programme of severe isolation and deprivations is the rule for most people on Death Row. They are locked up in solitary confinement, usually for twenty-three hours a day, and left to rot for years while the state tries to win the right to execute them through the appeal courts.

Once you have been sentenced to die in Pennsylvania, you are taken from the county jail and placed in solitary confinement inside a maximum-security prison run by the state. These places are designed to house the most violent and depraved convicts. In the first weeks of being sent to one of these, many men collapse under the stress of being left in such a black void. The isolation, coupled with the initiation rituals used by the guards to break them down mentally, proves just too much.

The administrations of these prisons actually endorse such efforts to 'break you' as, to them, a broken man goes along to get along. Therefore, you are left to fend for yourself from the outset.

For me, like everyone else, Death Row was a horror show from the very first day. My first placement in the state prison system was in State Correctional Institution (SCI) Graterford, located just outside of Philadelphia, where I was to be evaluated, or 'classified' as they put it, before being moved to a permanent prison to await execution.

In 1982, there was room for only twenty-four men to remain permanently at Graterford, because it had rather a small Restricted Housing Unit (or RHU), and I was told early on that I was not going to be one of those men. They did not want a high-profile case like mine in their prison and they did not like me. I was aggressive, had violent mood swings and was prone to outbursts. I even made a replica mini-electric chair out of cardboard and taped it to my bars in defiance.

It was while I was at Graterford waiting to learn where I would be housed permanently that I first heard the horror stories about SCI Huntingdon. Every man on Death Row in Graterford feared they might go to another prison in the future because they knew that more and more men were being sentenced to die across the state. If the staff did not like you or you caused trouble you were more likely to get shipped out to Huntingdon, in the central mountains of Pennsylvania, or the state penitentiary at Pittsburgh, on the other side of the state. Neither option was good. However, every time the subject came up in discussion between the men waiting to be evaluated for transfer, as I was, the same fear crept into their voices at the mere prospect of being selected to go to the worst place in the system: Huntingdon. No one wanted to find out just how bad it was. We knew that the men who had rioted at Graterford the previous year had been sent there, and rumours about what the guards had done to some militant Muslim prisoners, who had caused an uprising, were scary.

All I knew was that this was where I was definitely going, and I would be put on B-Block, where a Death Row had been created a few months before. To me it felt that the further away from Philadelphia I was sent, the more the reality of what was being done to me would sink in.

It was at 3.30 a.m. on 14 February 1983 that I was shouted awake by two guards standing in front of my cell with clubs and handcuffs. They told me that I was leaving for Huntingdon right now. I was taken out through the prison reception area and placed next to a large blue and yellow bus with metal screens over its windows parked beside the forty-foot rear wall. These prison buses were known to inmates as the 'Blue Birds', named after the bus manufacturer whose insignia was written on their sides. Now I saw four guards with huge piles of chains linking together a procession of men already in handcuffs. These were the other transfer prisoners, all waiting to be 'hooked up' to a partner for the ride. As a Death Row prisoner I was left separate, but an extra security device was used to attach my handcuffs to my belly chain.

I was shivering as I stood there in my handcuffs and leg irons, dressed only in a prison-issue yellow jumpsuit, lined up in the cold night air like a farm animal ready to be transported to the slaughter house. The other Huntingdon-destined prisoners and I were about to begin a nine-hour ride on a bus that no one wanted to go on, to a prison that no one wanted to be in. Any of the inmates on the bus who were headed for one of the state's other prisons just looked relieved not to be among us.

I kept to myself, trying to stay warm and get through all this without becoming motion sick – I had skipped breakfast, but even so I cannot ride on a bus without getting sick. I had been in one prison cell or another for over a year now and I was not ready for the movement of the bus as we rode along. However, I let the chatter from the others distract me from further thoughts of where I was heading.

The last stop for many of the gangsters who went from prison to prison acting tough, Huntingdon was legendary for the horrors done by its staff to its inmates. Even so, it was eerie how every man on that bus hushed as we made our way up the steep mountain back roads, closer and closer to our destination.

As soon as we pulled up inside the prison walls that afternoon, the guards emptied the bus of all the other men before four more guards climbed in and dragged me roughly from my seat. It all happened so fast that I had no time to brace myself for any of this. Next I was shoved up against a brick wall. All the guards were dressed in special, military-style outfits used to extract particularly violent prisoners or save hostages. Black gear and black uniforms. Three of them prodded their clubs into different points on my body while the other held my hands still by the cuffs. In the cold February sunshine outside of the building where Huntingdon's Death Row was located, just a few yards from where the bus was parked, I finally met its captain of the guards.

As he approached from between the men holding me with this quick military-style stride, he pulled up inches from my face and looked me hard in the eyes for a few lingering moments. As the man in charge of Death Row, one of the captains made it his personal business to literally get in the face of each new inmate. He loved being part of this place which revelled in its reputation as the hardest place in the prison system, and he loved the power he held over the lives of the 145 men housed on his block, or 'unit'. His voice was God-like to the men over whom he ruled.

His face still inches from mine, he began to address me in this very calm, detached voice: 'You're dead. Everyone you knew or loved is dead. Your family and everyone else who knew you are dead. And since *you* are dead, dead men do not speak in my unit, do you understand me?'

When he had finished I raised my head and said a soft 'Yes, sir' in reply.

He backhanded me with his right hand across my face so hard and so quickly that it rocked me. Suddenly I saw bright points of light in my left eye where he had smacked me with his clenched knuckles. From my jaw to my eye, my face filled with heat where I'd been hit, and my left ear was ringing from the blow. I pulled myself upright and managed to hang on to my balance as I tried to brace myself for what might happen next. I stood absolutely still and waited without looking at anything.

But I never got to do or say anything else because now he turned from me and said over his shoulder to the four guards holding me: 'Thirty seconds.'

I had no clue what this meant, but it was clearly the words these men had been waiting for. Instantly they were on me, their clubs flying, as, over the next half-minute, I was beaten so mercilessly that I was grateful to be knocked unconscious after the first few blows. They beat me all along the backs of my legs, from my butt to my feet. They tore into my calves and thighs and really worked on my lower back and buttocks. These men were professionals; they knew exactly what they had to do – a beating which would leave the prisoner in as much pain as possible but without breaking any bones.

I learned later that this captain 'fed' his officers a new inmate once a week for them to take out their lives' frustrations on. It was also his way of controlling random violence by these same guards, who might otherwise have acted alone and targeted anyone they felt like. In the past at Huntingdon it had all been too chaotic to let the guards just randomly go wild and so, the administration reasoned, it was better that the guards were given 'sacrifices' on which to perform 'controlled' beatings than for them to become predatory and out of control. I was told all this soon after I arrived by the inmate in the exercise cage next to mine when we were allowed out for our thirty minutes of exercise a day – the one occasion on which we were allowed to talk without being harmed for it. However, I could not have cared less what the intention behind it was when I became that week's 'sacrifice'.

I had prepared myself as best I could for how, as a convicted rapist-murderer, I was likely to be dealt with, yet what truly shocked me, right after the beating I got, were the actions of the medical staff who worked in this insane place. Having been dragged unconscious into my first cell on Death Row and given a little extra beating because I came to temporarily and was struggling against them in my semi-conscious state, I was 'examined' by the nurse on duty. She stood outside my cell with a guard beside her no more than a few minutes after I had come to, and called me to the window by saying my new prison number and my last name in a loud, official voice. Without even looking at me or caring if I answered her, she read from the clipboard in front of her. On it was a single sheet of paper, the routine document the prison provided for her to read aloud to every new inmate.

Among other things, she explained how I was to follow set procedures for seeing a doctor should I 'think' I needed one. The guard standing next to her felt this was the point at which to laugh, given the obvious pain I was in.

But, no matter how much it hurt me to do so, I stood up on my wobbly legs by my cell window and willed this nurse to look at me. I was praying that I could stand upright long enough for her to see my swollen eye and the trickle of blood from my nose. On the side of my face there was a large mark the shape of a left boot, grooved into my skin, where one of the guards had stood on my face while the others had removed my handcuffs and leg irons, ripping my arms up behind me as high as they would go. Now I deliberately refused to say anything just so that the nurse would have to look at me as she rattled through the questions on her clipboard. When she got no replies, the guard next to her added in an annoyed voice, 'Inmate makes no response.'

Then, without ever looking up from her clipboard, the nurse just walked off. It was as if that was all she wanted to see. I felt as if I was no more of a human being to her than a cardboard cut-out placed in that cell. Now I truly knew what it was like to be regarded as non-human by people I didn't even know.

I felt sick and light-headed, and my side was aching from where I had been kicked in the ribs, so I just let my grasp slip from the bars of my cell window and slid down the wall as painlessly as I could. I could not believe that I had been openly assaulted for no reason by the guards and that the healthcare professional who was meant to look after me had just totally ignored it all. I doubted I could live in this place for long. What kind of human being could? Some of the men I met when I first got there had been in the RHU for ten years or more. How was I ever going to keep from going insane in this madhouse?

I hardly slept that first week on Death Row as I kept waiting for the guards to come into my cell and attack me again. I could hear men whimper or cry out in the night. And the sound I came to know so well was the one of someone else being dragged into the housing unit and left in another empty cell for the nurse to come by with her clipboard interview. This was nothing like I had imagined the prison to be, and nothing in the world of which I had previously been a part had prepared me for such a brutal existence.

When that captain of the guards said that dead men were not allowed to speak in his unit, he meant exactly that. If the guards caught you talking to another inmate in a nearby cell, you got a written misconduct report and they confiscated whatever possessions you had. The next time they caught you talking out loud, they had four officers rush into your cell wearing protective armour, beat you down with clubs and hold you steady while the nurse on duty came in and stabbed you in the butt with a needle full of psychotropic drugs – usually 100 mg of a drug called Thorazine. It's really creepy how a normally functioning man can converse with you in a lucid way in the exercise cage next to you one day and the next time you see him he has become a zombie who doesn't even recognise you.

For those men who persisted with their bad behaviours after drug treatment there was the ultimate torment, the dreaded 'Glass Bubble'. The Glass Bubble was, in reality, just a regular cell that had had the solid red bricks of its front wall replaced by glass bricks. This allowed the guards to see the prisoner at all times but also, more importantly, those bricks acted as a sound block, so the cell was completely hushed. Then the lights were left on twenty-four hours a day, and positioned on a chair outside was a guard whose job it was to make sure that the inmate was woken every twenty minutes or so for a 'head count'.

Day after day the inmate was forced to partake in this same 'standing count' process. Usually after four to five days of this sort of sleep deprivation he would lose all awareness of time and place. The guards called the process 'waiting for the white-out', because inmates who lived through it sometimes described how their eyes would see only this sort of ultra-bright light and nothing else. It is much like becoming snow blind, I would imagine.

And so, while the rules are being forced on him in these most brutal of ways, a prisoner somehow has to find the courage and will to fight his appeals and seek to survive. I was so angry those first few years I was in Huntingdon that I would sometimes beat my head against the wall just to feel physical pain. I wanted to use my anger to keep me alive, because I saw what happens when men stop fighting. It hurts to think of them even now.

I was sitting on the bed in my ground-floor cell reading a newspaper only a few months into my time at Huntingdon when I witnessed my first suicide. A prisoner housed on the top tier, two floors above me and about three cells along, simply dived head-first off the balcony. As soon as they opened his cell door to take him for his shower, he jumped, handcuffs still on, over the railing. I had no idea what had happened. I just heard the sound of what I thought was a mattress being thrown out of a cell on to the floor thirty feet below. (The plastic mattresses on the bed sometimes had to be removed if a diseased inmate had died in his cell.) But when I stood up and walked over to my cell door to see what it was, I saw him lying there.

He was a black man, in his thirties I guessed, but even though he was lying on his chest his face was angled unnaturally upwards. Urine and blood pooled about his lower body as he twitched uncontrollably and then stopped. I could not have been more than twelve feet away from him, yet he looked so unreal that I really did not process the fact that I was looking at a dead human being until the guards came and covered his face with a towel.

The man who had jumped to his death had served fifteen years there, the last four in that cell almost directly above me. How in the world did anyone handle four years of this type of craziness? I had only been there for a few months and already I could not see myself living like this, with no end in sight. This thought was soon becoming the worst thought in my head. I came back into my cell from the exercise cages one day soon after that inmate jumped and looked at all that I was allowed to possess. A few paper sacks full of legal materials, some novels I had managed to barter for, some cheap toiletries and a small radio – that was all I owned. I thought about how that man had been driven to take his own life and he was not even on Death Row – he was just a prisoner who had broken the rules four years earlier. I was not going to last even that long unless I became stronger than I could ever have dreamed myself capable of.

Over the next twenty years, I watched as eleven men hanged themselves, swallowed razor blades, cut their own throats or just jumped to their deaths as that first man had done. Although I honestly do not know how I survived decades during which death was a welcomed relief from the endless madness, I do believe that one motivating factor that helped me not fall into the life-sucking horror of the place was given to me by my father.

My parents only got to see me twice a year, as they lived hundreds of miles away and could not afford to come more often than that, so each year they came once for my birthday in May and again at Christmas. It was during one of these visits that my father, a proud man, simply turned to me and said: 'I cannot do anything for you.'

In that moment I looked into the eyes of someone who had no hope for me whatsoever. There was such complete bleakness in his face that I swallowed every bit of pride I had and swore before God that I was going to do whatever it took, not only to survive but also to try and become the redeeming face of love for him and for my family. I told him, 'I am going to try to do whatever it takes to come home, Pop.'

I went back into my cell that day determined to grow strong enough to keep my word to my father.

8 Meet your new attorney

The death sentence imposed on me for the kidnapping, rape and murder of Linda Mae Craig mandated an automatic review of my case on appeal before the State Supreme Court of Pennsylvania. Any prisoner sentenced to death in Pennsylvania is assured of two things: a first-time appeal before the state's highest court and a court-appointed attorney to represent him on appeal.

I think it became clear early on that my trial attorney, Sam Stretton, was not going to stay on for the appeals. Appeals cost money and my family had scraped together all they could to pay him to represent me in the two trials that I had faced in 1982. Sam would have had to represent me at his own expense and I could not reasonably expect him to do this, so it was best for all concerned if I had someone else present my case on appeal. The state pays attorneys picked by the local court to handle such appeals from a list of lawyers in the area. All I could hope for was that I would be assigned a lawyer who was competent and who would listen to me when I tried to convince him or her that I was actually innocent.

It wasn't until December 1983 that I met the first appellate attorney who was to represent me for my direct appeal against my conviction for the murder of Mrs Craig. His name was Mr Joseph Bullen.

I was in my first full year at Huntingdon when I met him. The previous months of being forced to live in silence meant that I had to fight hard not to succumb to the anger I felt each day at being denied the right just to voice my thoughts in my own cell. I had also been beaten by the guards for talking out loud and I felt humiliated at being deprived of the right to communicate with others. I would just sit in my cell and watch those guards and wonder how they had become so cold. It was clear that, having spent many years abusing other human beings, all they could do now was keep a routine. It was as if they had to make sure that they were being as cruel and petty as possible at every opportunity. I got a kick in the legs when I was being moved from my cell and I got a slap if I looked too hard at a guard.

I was being affected deeply by this daily ritual of petty abuse and it was beginning to make me bitter. I always seemed to have to be on my guard against the next little trick they might pull. The thought of living like this for years on end, as well as trying to fight the death penalty, was draining me and I really wanted a ray of hope to come from this new attorney.

Yet my initial meeting with the man appointed by the courts to represent me on appeal was so unlike what I had expected. One afternoon I was told that I had a visitor. I was taken out of my cell and brought in handcuffs to one of the two small 'attorney's booths' located at the rear of the prison's main visiting room. It was my first official attorney visit and I was anxious to meet my new lawyer. The room was just five feet square, divided down the middle by a screen and glass barrier that ran down from the ceiling to the floor. All Death Row prisoners had to use these two rooms for all their visits, regardless of who they were seeing, as we were allowed no physical contact.

So I was sitting there in this empty room, waiting for whoever was going to come through the small outside visitors' door, when in marched this balding, portly middle-aged man in a dark green suit. Before he had even sat down, though, he started by referring to a letter he had written to me prior to the visit. In that letter, he said, he had explained that he had not chosen to take on my case but had been appointed by the judge – and before we got any further he wanted to make this point very clear. When I in turn began to introduce myself he interrupted me immediately: 'Hold off saying anything. There are three very important things you must know.'

I willed myself to sit still but I looked him hard in the face as it became clear that this man was here to make some points that I was not going to like. The first thing he wanted me to know, he began, was that it was a waste of time for both of us if I was going to keep trying to convince him that I was innocent. Having reviewed the case file and the whole transcript from my court records, it was his opinion that the state had presented a fair case against me and I was guilty. He said all this without even flinching as he stared me right in my face.

I bit hard on my lip to keep quiet as he moved deftly on to point number two.

He was a high-ranking official in the Army reserves, he continued; he had always been a supporter of the death penalty and his only concern was that executions were carried out within the rule of law. He would therefore see to it that my appeals were all presented according to law.

I was not really sure what he meant by that bit about it all being 'according to law', but then again I was still feeling angry over his first point – that he had basically just called me a rapist and a murderer to my face.

Mr Bullen then surprised me by saying that his third point was that he had been appointed by the trial judge, Judge Robert Kelly (for whom, he quickly added, he had considerable personal respect), and so, despite his own views, he was meeting me now in his official capacity as my new attorney to discuss any 'issues' that I may wish to discuss with him relating to the appeal for which he had already filed.

It took a long few moments for my pulse to slow down enough for me to say anything. I was stung by his directness. And if it wasn't such a serious moment, I think I would have burst out laughing at this impressively rehearsed performance. Instead, a feeling of stubbornness welled up inside me as I replied, 'Thank you for hearing my side of things before you make up your mind about what you file on my behalf.'

Then, before he could say anything, I added: 'Your letter says that you have already filed my appeal, so if you know I am guilty and you have read the files, why have you come here?'

His only response to my question was to ask another question: 'Well, is there anything you can tell me that is going to change my mind about what I have read in the case files and trial transcripts?'

He looked at me just willing me to come out firing at him a whole list of things that had been improperly handled legally. He was braced for me to tell him what laws or rules had not been followed during my trial and he *so* wanted me to tell him how wrong he had been about my guilt. Then, seemingly out of nowhere, I just began:

'Here's something I can tell you all about that's not in your case files or in the trial transcripts. I am twenty-two years old. There is only one other guy on Death Row who's younger than me right now, so mostly it's all older men in here.'

An unsure look came over Mr Bullen's face. What did all this have to do with my telling him something hugely impor-tant that was not in the records? But he allowed me to go on, comfortable in the expectation that he would be ready for whatever I had to say.

I continued: 'So I am like this sort of young "eye candy" to every pervert in here who sees all of this blond hair on my head and how young-looking I am, you know? And then, when I go to the shower I have to make sure to keep my boxer shorts on while we all wash up together in this huge room that they march us into six at a time for our five-minute shower.'

Nothing. As I stood talking to him from my side of the room, Mr Bullen just sat looking up at me from his chair, blank-faced, waiting to see where I was going with all this. I went on: 'I really wonder if you know what it's like to have men touch themselves openly while they are looking at you, and you are unable to do anything about it . . . because, first of all, they are all maniac murderers who will kill you if they can. Then, of course, there are also a dozen guards standing nearby holding clubs who will beat your head in if you do anything they decide is "aggressive".'

Mr Bullen folded his arms comfortably across his chest. It was his little gesture of confidence, as if to show that if I intended to appeal to him by describing how horrible prison conditions were, then he was going to enjoy my failure.

But as he sat there, arms folded, all ready and waiting for what he thought was going to be a litany of complaints, I also relaxed and grew more comfortable in the contest in which we now found ourselves engaged.

'So, anyway, last month I was sitting at the metal desk bolted to the wall in my cell. I was writing a letter and minding my own business when the inmate trustee who sweeps up the cell block came by. He used his broom to push a note under my door that another prisoner had asked him to give to me. When I picked up this folded-up bit of paper I had no idea what it was at first. After having checked that no guard was around, I opened it up and saw on it a hand-written note.

'"Dear Nit," it began, followed by some words I could hardly read. It took me a moment to decipher the spelling and realise what the author of the note was after. He wanted me to write sex letters for him to masturbate to. In exchange he offered me twenty dollars a week, which he promised would be paid into my prison account by one of his family members from the outside.'

Mr Bullen sat rigid, with distaste at the obvious homo-sexual references but also drawn, despite himself, by the sick retelling of what life was really like in this place.

Despite the lack of space, I tried pacing up and down on my side of the room before continuing: 'When I first read the note I got really angry and I wanted to shout out from my cell at this sick pervert and say just what I thought of his note. I wanted others to know what he was like, too, but then I also knew that the guards would just beat my head in for yelling, so I didn't. What was particularly frustrating to me was that I got that note on a Friday afternoon, so I would have to wait until Monday morning to have a chance to talk to anybody about it out in the exercise yard. You see, Mr Bullen, we are only allowed out on weekdays for our thirty minutes of exercise in these dog kennel-like cages behind the Death Row building – although I wouldn't put a full-sized animal in a cage like the ones they make us use.'

Throughout all this Mr Bullen just continued to sit with his arms folded, letting me go on. He was sure I was complaining now.

I picked up momentum as I went on: 'I was really angry that this moron prisoner who sent me the note couldn't even spell my name correctly, or that he thought that just because I am so young he could approach me with this homosexual bullshit. I couldn't wait to go out into those cages that Monday and tell someone what this guy had done.'

When I got to this point, I sat down directly in front of Mr Bullen and finished with the following lines, delivered in a quick monotone, introspective and a bit deflated-sounding:

'And you know what, Mr Bullen? I end up getting placed in the end cage right next to Stevie Lloyd! Man, out of all the guys I live with in here I get stuck in the cage right next to crazy-ass Stevie Lloyd! You know who he is, don't ya?'

Mr Bullen shook his head, 'No.'

'Stevie Lloyd is in here because he has this fixation with stealing horses. Stevie loves horses and he goes on and on about all sorts of horses and what he'd like to do to them if you'd let him. Also, he always talks about himself as Stevie and, you know, Mr Bullen, when someone refers to themself in the third person it can really be annoying. It can be especially bad, Mr Bullen, when they also have a cleft palette and they spray spittle from their mouth every time they say a word that begins with the letter "S".'

A little stunned at this new turn in my story, Mr Bullen was clearly not at all sure what, if anything, this had to do with my appeal and he was looking at me curiously.

'Now, with Stevie in particular, it's difficult to handle because he has missing and rotten teeth in the front of his mouth so his spittle can be real nasty when he gets you. Everyone who can, tries to stay a few feet back when Stevie talks.' I saw Mr Bullen flinch. I was starting to annoy him now with my smartass tone of voice, but I was also beginning to feel empowered by his finally starting to show painful responses to what I was saying.

Quickly I moved in for the big finish: 'But I took my chances, Mr Bullen, and I just walked over to the fence separating our two cages and said: "Yo, Stevie, come here and listen to this, man!"

'"Stevie is busy."

'"Yeah well, get your ass un-busy and come over here real quick!"

'"What you got for Stevie?"

'"Man, listen. I was sitting there Friday when that worker 'Flat-top' comes by and shoves a note under my door. It was a note from 'Big Deek', ya know?"

'"Yeah, yeah, Stevie know."

'"So, I am trying to read through all his misspelled words in the note and it soon turns out that this sick fucker wants me to write him sex letters! Now Stevie, I know *you* know I'm not gay and that sick bastard has a lot of nerve to ask me to write him stuff like this. It's wrong! Stevie, what kind of shit is that, where this guy thinks he can ask me to write him some dirty shit so he can masturbate to it and I am not supposed to get angry or try to hurt him, just because he's a lifer? The sicko had the nerve to tell me he would have his sister send $20 a week to my account if I went along with this scheme of his, too!"'

A short silence, then with bewilderment on my face I revealed to Mr Bullen what Stevie had told me: '"Stevie got the same note."

'That stopped me. "Really, you got the same note from Big Deek asking you to write him sex letters?"

'He repeated: "Stevie got same note, too. Stevie got offered $25 a week."

'Mr Bullen, when Stevie stopped me cold by telling me how he got the same offer but better to write sex letters, do you know what I said? I said: "That's fucking bullshit, Stevie, you got all those pockmarks on your face and you got those nasty teeth. How the hell did you get offered more money than me, when I am much better looking than you?"

'Stevie was stung by my outburst, Mr Bullen, and he said that he had been offered more money than me because he had a good reputation for writing letters as he'd written some for another prisoner which had made the man really think that it was a woman writing them. Stevie said that he always made sure that when he wrote sex letters for money to another prisoner, he used the guy's name when he described having an orgasm. Also that just because I had nice blond hair and a cute ass, it did not mean he was ugly and he really did not want to talk to me any further.'

Then, working up to my theme, I continued: 'You know what Stevie Lloyd taught me that day, Mr Bullen? Stevie taught me that even someone who murders other human beings or has an obvious mental disorder like Stevie Lloyd is just as valuable in prison as someone like me who has a really nice full head of blond hair and a firm young ass!'

I drew a breath before delivering my final flurry. I knew Mr Bullen would be angry now and I wanted to get it all in before he had had enough.

'As a matter of fact, after Stevie told me that he had been offered more money than me for writing sex letters, I admit that I felt angered. I felt slighted that I was not given the better offer simply because I was much better looking than him. Then I realised that maybe Stevie should be writing my appeals out for me, because at least I know he cares enough about me that he is willing to use my actual name when describing how *he* would fuck me the way *you* are!'

I was into high-energy shouting mode by this time. Joe Bullen jumped to his feet as I ended my performance and began cramming the legal papers neatly stacked on the counter into a thick leather case he had pulled out from under the table. He was red-faced, trying to get out of the room as quickly as he could, but I just smiled and laughed at him. Then I really let him have it. 'Come on, Joe, it's not like we can't still be friends, buddy!'

Mr Bullen stopped cramming papers into his case long enough to stare at me before saying, 'I hope they fuckin' fry your sick ass.'

My jaw tightened in anger at what he said, but my eyes were clear of the feelings that I could barely contain. I gave a taunting salute and began a mock march.

Having gotten all of his papers into the case and snapped the flap shut, Mr Bullen just stopped long enough to say, in a very official-sounding voice, 'I feel sorry for you, Nick Yarris, you really are making your parents so proud!'

At this I lost all composure. I wanted to get in my retort before he left the room. I was also in mid breath, which made me end up sounding a bit off key as I shouted: 'Hey, you used my first name! Does that mean that when you write me your next letter telling me how you lost my appeal, you will also include some sex stuff that I can sell to "Deek the Freak" for $20!'

The door closed as the last of my words beat out the snap of the lock. I sat there listening through the walls as Mr Bullen's footsteps faded from the outer room.

In the fifteen minutes it took for officers to come and bring me back to my prison cell, I sat there in that empty room and laughed my ass off at the pig-headed way Bullen had acted. Then I cried at how I had just dashed all the hopes my family had pinned on my new lawyer.

And then I laughed again at my own will to fight for myself, knowing that I was going to face a pointless end. And then, finally, I cried some more as I realised that, while I sat there laughing today, whatever pleasure I had gotten from taunting that man I was going to pay for many times over.

9 How *not* to escape from Death Row

The incredible events leading up to my trial and imprisonment were about to be added to in a big way. I was not
really ready for what happened next, which can only be
described as bizarre. And yet, in comparison to the world
in which I was already lost, perhaps it was not as far-fetched
as all that.

Mr Bullen had filed my appeal 'according to law', just as
he said he would, and, much to everyone's surprise, his
appeal had been taken seriously by the State Supreme
Court. In March 1984 I was granted a hearing to determine
why so much of the homicide file had gone missing prior to
my trial. This 'remand' effectively drew attention to all of
the errors and deliberate withholdings of the evidence. It
did not mean I would automatically be granted anything,
but it was the first positive thing that had happened to me.
I guess, whatever I felt about the cold professionalism of Joe
Bullen, he did what he was trained as a lawyer to do: he gave
me a fighting chance. And if I could get the trial record to
reflect the fact that numerous pages of the homicide file had

been destroyed or withheld, I was hopeful that a new trial would be ordered.

As part of this, I braced myself for that woeful effort it takes to find hope when no one seems to be a friend or ally. Mr Bullen orchestrated for me to have a remand hearing in early 1985. In this regard, I allowed him to have a psychiatrist, Perry Berman, examine me for the purpose of seeking to have my death sentence set aside because I was mentally impaired.

I bristled at having this done to me, but I was very young and I felt unable to fend off Mr Bullen's management of both me and my court case. I lied constantly to my parents, telling them that he was doing all these really significant things that we would be able to use in court to overturn the convictions. At every chance I buoyed up their hopes while keeping quiet about the tensions between the lawyer and myself. Meanwhile, I prepared as best I could for the hearing before Judge Kelly. This time I was to be prosecuted by a man named Dennis McAndrews. I had no idea who he was, but I expected him to be no less vicious than Barry Gross, the man who had sent me to Death Row with such gusto.

I also knew that Mr Bullen had approached my mother prior to the hearing, asking her to convince me to dismiss my appeals and accept a 'deal' wherein I would be offered life imprisonment. My mother told me on the phone that when he'd said this she had replied, 'Mr Bullen, I would rather see my son executed for something he did not do, because I was there and I looked that boy in his face at 4.30 p.m. on December the 15th, 1981, and no one is going to make *me* say otherwise!'

I had no idea what lay ahead for me. All I could hope was that we had put together a strong enough case that the Supreme Court would see how badly flawed my original trial had been. But what happened next was as sudden and outlandish as anything I could ever have dreamed of.

On 15 February 1985 I became one of the USA's most hunted human beings when I escaped from custody. My escape was splashed across the evening news on national television and radio. Residents of the Delaware Valley region of Pennsylvania and all of Philadelphia were warned that a dangerous criminal was on the run. Over 200 police and federal enforcement agency officers were involved in the five-and-a-half-hour chase, which began at 5.30 that evening.

As I ran through woods in freezing temperatures, wearing only a set of prison-issue clothes and some stiff leather shoes, which had been loaned to me for the trip, I was in agony. A helicopter circled above me and hundreds of police chased me as I ran as fast as I could. By 10 p.m. I was exhausted and badly damaged from my efforts to outrun the police. I had no intention of escaping from anywhere when I had left the prison earlier that day and here I was stumbling blindly through some woods getting ripped from the thorns.

It had all begun in the most innocuous way. Because my appeal had been successful, I was being transferred from

Huntingdon prison to Delaware County jail, nearly 275 miles away, for the court hearing. I was sitting cuffed behind a security barrier in the back seat of the police car and the two deputy sheriffs with me were armed, but we were friendly enough. They must have been looking forward to the long, relaxed trip with all expenses paid, plus overtime. I was their only charge and I knew both men from my original journeys to jail and back from the county courtroom three years earlier.

I had never had any problems with these two guys, who were both over sixty. They were only trying to do their jobs, handling as best they could the broken human cargo that the justice system deals with. I chatted with them amiably as we drove along. When we stopped for fuel at the beginning of the four-hour ride to Delaware County jail they even bought me a cold can of soda, which I held in my cuffed hands and sipped through a straw.

As we left the major interstate road in Chester County, just thirty miles from our destination, one of the officers asked me if I needed to use the men's room. I said that I did and we stopped at the Hess gas station near the town of Exton, Pennsylvania. The restrooms at the station were set away from the fuel pumps, in a building not much more than twenty by thirty feet, with two black-door cubicles, one for men, the other for women, side by side. For some unexplainable reason, the officer driving the patrol car drove past the restrooms and parked the car out of sight of the building, about forty yards away. This one simple act caused the drama that was to unfold that bitterly cold evening.

The three of us got out of the car and we all walked briskly to the men's room. As I stood at the urinal, I did not know that the driver had drifted back to the car, leaving me alone with his partner, who stood holding the door for me. Nor did I know that this officer would have the sudden urge to urinate, having listened to me. I just turned and started to make the shivering dash back to the car while thinking I was being guided by his ever-present hands, always on me when I was moved.

The officer waiting by the car saw none of this. I did not realise that the other deputy wasn't behind me and the surprised sheriff in front of me had no idea that his partner was simply using the men's room. And I had no idea that, on seeing me turn the corner without his partner guiding me by the arm, he would panic.

When our eyes met he put his right hand reassuringly on his gun. That was enough to send a bolt of fear straight through me. We were only three feet apart. I had no idea why he was feeling for his gun, but in the split second that I looked into his frightened eyes, I bolted.

Before I could stop myself, he had fired the first of two point-blank shots at me. My hands were still cuffed in front of me as I stumbled and fell down the embankment next to the toilet block. The flesh ripped from my palms as I used my hands to break my fall. I felt the percussion of the blast from the deputy's gun. He fired again as I picked myself up.

He was yelling to his partner for help, but the man didn't come out of the toilet. He must have heard the shots and decided to stay put. When I stood up I saw the huge plate-glass window of a fast-food restaurant in front of me and I ran at it, as if to jump straight through it. This stopped the deputy from shooting at me again. Presumably the chance of hitting innocent diners was too great a risk. My efforts paid off as my scared legs propelled me out of gun sight long enough for me to turn the corner and flee.

The alarm sounded as the two deputies regrouped and started to search for me. I ran for about 300 yards back along the road we had just driven down, but then turned right at the first major intersection, and then right again after running another 300 yards, back towards my pursuers. When, having made this circle, I was within 100 yards of the spot where I had just escaped, I hid in some bushes, watching, as one of the policemen called for help on the patrol car radio.

For a second I wanted to give myself up before the situation got out of hand. But I was all shaken up. Both my hamstrings were torn from my fall and my hands were bleeding badly. I started to vomit, then hyperventilate as I lay there on the frozen ground. I was scared and a bit delirious.

As my body heat dropped I also began to convulse and shiver, but I forced myself to focus on the situation I was in. I slid off the plastic coating from the arm of my eyeglasses, inserted the metal rod into the lock of my handcuffs and freed the catch. (In three years of being handcuffed every day the one thing I knew about was how to undo cuffs. You learn a lot of things from your captors, I now realised.) With my arms free, I crawled along on my knees and elbows. I was amazed at how fast it had all happened. I hadn't intended to escape at all; I had simply reacted to the deputy reaching for his gun.

After crawling along for about 200 yards I saw some sort of police station with squad cars driving away from it, presumably in search of me. I decided that this would be the perfect place to hide. Only later did I find out that it was the Whitehall Municipal Police Building, where the police soon set up a command post. In my mind I silently asked myself, 'Who would search for a Death Row prisoner behind a police station?' When no more police officers seemed to be coming out of the station, I scrambled across the parking lot. Then I hid behind the large green trash dumpsters. This was a good move until, an hour later, the cold really started to set in. In the dark I had stepped in some freezing water in those awful stiff prison shoes and I really needed to get out of my hiding place. I was cramping and I was beginning to have hypothermic convulsions.

I chose my moment and darted out, running right out behind the tail lights of a patrol car. But I was so sure I had been seen by the driver of that car that I panicked and cut off to the woods nearby.

I started to run on my badly damaged legs, feeling the flesh of my feet split open with each step. I knew I was at the limits of my endurance as I pushed myself to keep going. But I also felt weirdly detached. I was able to block out the searing pain in my hands and burst feet.

Then I saw the light of a helicopter as it approached in the night sky. I ran for the biggest tree I could find and hugged it tightly as the helicopter circled above me. I darted off to the side of an apartment complex and the helicopter went the other way. Then I ran in the opposite direction for as long as I could before crawling under a truck parked in this big construction site. I hid there under that truck for an hour until once again I had to move because of the cold.

Having failed to steal a van from in front of a pizza store, I spotted a mall parking lot and decided to run for it. Again the helicopter got involved in the chase. Luckily for me, though, its infrared camera wasn't working – it must have broken down in the cold – so the helicopter's pilot could only use his huge spotlight to shine down on me, but he couldn't find me.

Next, I ran on to some railroad tracks, where I lay still for what felt like ages, too scared to move. Eventually, though, the helicopter pilot gave up and moved off, so I decided to walk along the railroad tracks. I was so delirious with pain that I was blubbering as I stepped gingerly along the rail line, whilst also punching my legs to keep the pain fresh so that I would keep moving. I crept along those tracks stepping over the wooden railroad ties one at a time until at last I could no longer hear that helicopter sound that scared me so much.

By 10.30 p.m., having walked for over three hours heading north, I arrived at the deserted train station of Frazer, Pennsylvania. I cried and cursed all the way, but somehow I made it.

There, I hot-wired a 1965 Ford Mustang sitting in the parking lot and started driving towards Philadelphia, trying to figure out what to do next.

As I drove along I listened to the local news station and ate some candy I'd found in the glove compartment. I was exhausted and badly injured, but too scared to sleep. I had no money and no idea what to do next. My escape was all over the news station. They made me out to be some deranged psychotic killer who was on Death Row for murdering a woman who looked like the girl who had jilted him. Women in particular were warned to stay inside, while the public at large were told that I was considered extremely dangerous, as I had already been sentenced to death and so had nothing to lose.

I knew that nobody would believe me if I told them what had really happened, that I hadn't intended to escape at all. And I had absolutely no hope of beating the entire law enforcement community of the United States of America. How could my life have been so completely blown to bits? Convicted of the rape and murder of a woman I'd never met, now I was being hunted by every police officer in the country. How was I ever going to survive?

I found a coin on the seat of the car I had stolen and used it to call one of my sisters who had recently married and moved to a new house in south-west Philadelphia. She agreed to let me come to her house and get bandages, money and clothes. I reckoned that, as she had just moved house, in the few hours after my escape the police were unlikely to have figured out where she lived in order to put a watch on it. At 6 a.m. I walked up to her front door and knocked quietly. My sister opened the door with her daughter in her arms. She gave me $200, a hat, a pair of winter gloves and some bandages for my badly ripped-up hands. Soon I was on my way to New York City, two hours' drive away.

When I got to New York I drove to the Lower East Side of Manhattan, where I abandoned the car and went in search of a low-rent motel room. I was lucky in that I found a street person who showed me where to get a room for $7 a night. Then I went out and bought lunchmeat and rolls and a huge box of Epsom salts. Over the next three days I spent hours at a time sitting in a bath of warm salt water. I was not physically able to walk for more than a few steps – my feet had cuts going along the length of them from just below the big toe back to the heel. When I walked it made the flesh grind on itself and I was in so much pain I just wept. But I forced myself to let my body heal itself as much as it could.

Five days after my escape, I went outside for the first time since I'd checked into the motel room. As I stepped out into the cold night air I half expected the police to jump me at any second. I willed myself not to look other people in the face and turned away from the cars on the street. At one point I saw a police car and ducked into a store to buy some food while nervously looking at my photo on some of the daily papers still on the shelves. I stayed out only a short while, as I had a headache from the noise and the cold temperature. Once my legs worked better I ventured out again to buy some cheap clothes, underwear and trainers from the Salvation Army store. I was down to my last few dollars and soon I was on the lookout for things to steal.

I ended up taking a man's wallet and using his credit cards to purchase a plane ticket to Orlando, Florida. In 1985 you did not need identification to get on board an internal flight in the USA. I simply took a taxi to LaGuardia airport and soon I was on my way to Florida on a 757 jet. As I flew out of NYC I looked out at the city below.

What next? I wanted to believe that I could be smart enough and strong enough to handle the constant fear that I might be recaptured at any moment, but inside I knew that this was all some huge mistake which was going to keep on unravelling.

On arriving in Florida I simple-mindedly hatched a very straightforward plan: I would rob some drug dealers and make enough money to leave the country. I was already familiar with Florida, having been there as a young tearaway, and its thriving drug trade was well known; the fact that I knew no one did not strike me as important. Somehow I would steal enough cash to leave the USA for good.

Then the reality set in. I couldn't get the identity documents I needed to travel. I couldn't find any big-time drug dealers to rob. And I was not holding up too well to the fear that I could be gunned down by a policeman at any second. I was staying in a cheap hotel in Orlando, trapped in a weird mental state. One minute I was terrified that I would be recognised; the next I would temporarily forget that I was on the FBI's 'Ten Most Wanted' list and override my fear. Soon I was talking to girls, going into restaurants and walking around openly. I had changed my hair and gotten new glasses, so soon I had a sense of not being myself any more, and it began to play tricks with my mind. I adopted the 'role' of Daniel Joseph Corbett, a name I had taken from a graveyard in one of my attempts to get identification. Underneath it all, though, I was just incredibly lonely and desperate to talk to anyone. I had just spent the past three years in solitary confinement in Huntingdon prison and suddenly here I was on a beach, looking at attractive women walking by in bikinis, just one more 23-year-old guy among thousands.

I had to fight to keep aware that one slip and I would be sending myself back to hell. Just one person seeing me and recalling my face and it was all over. Yet I also desperately wanted to talk and smile and be normal. The constant emotional rollercoaster ride was killing me. I had met a girl and started to see her, only to be caught in so many lies that she didn't want to have anything to do with me after two dates. The pressure to distinguish what was really happening from my own version of reality was growing, and I was cracking. I was so sure I was going to die now that I was even beginning to feel that prison was the safest place for me and here on the beaches of Florida were the worst minefields imaginable. I longed just to call my mom and hear her voice, let her know I was OK.

As each day passed I edged closer and closer to the choice I felt I had to make. Either I must hand myself in, go back to prison and continue to work to prove my innocence or I must kill myself in a way that no one would ever find me – that way, at least, my family would never have to see me in chains again. I did not want to die, but nor did I want to go back to Huntingdon. Finally, though, I realised that I could not bring myself to commit suicide. This was going to be one of the hardest things I would ever face in my life, but I was going to have to go back to Death Row.

And that is exactly what I did. I was given my chance when I was stopped by the local Florida police, who had no idea who I was. On 10 March 1985 there was a domestic disturbance at the hotel I had been staying in at Daytona Beach. The police had been called and were stopping cars leaving the hotel, including mine. The police found the pistol I had hidden under a towel sitting on the passenger seat and arrested and booked me under the false name I had adopted of Daniel Joseph Corbett.

Since I had given them no social security number and no identification the police assigned me a $5,000 bail for possession of a weapon and driving a stolen car and put me in a holding cell at the Valusia County jail. I had $8,500 in stolen cash on me when I was arrested but, because of the drug confiscation laws in Florida covering large sums of cash, the money was also put into holding. Still, all I had to do was call a bail bondsman using the money as a deposit for my release and I could get myself out. I was about to do just that when I picked up the phone in the holding cell – and called my father instead.

'I can't do this, Pop, I can't keep running,' I said.

'Are you sure?' is all he asked.

'Yeah, I wanna come back.'

Once I told my father where I was, he hung up the phone and immediately called the FBI in Philadelphia to tell them where they could find me. He asked them to come and get me quickly, before I changed my mind.

Soon there was a large crowd of jail staff in the holding cell ready to escort me over to the maximum security unit. The warden was amazed that I hadn't bailed out and walked away. I didn't have the energy to tell him that I was actually innocent and all I wanted was to be given the chance to prove it. I just tried to spare myself the agony of telling them why I was turning myself in, while at the same time realising that I would have to plead guilty to what I had done out on the run, and that would really mess up my appeals.

On my twenty-fourth birthday, 17 May 1985, I was sentenced to an additional 35-year sentence for robbery and gun possession in Florida: I confessed to robbing a drug dealer in Orlando who later told the police what I had done. Now I was to be housed for four months on Florida's Death Row, next to some of America's most notorious murderers in the 'East Unit' of Florida State Prison (FSP) Raiford, before being sent back to Pennsylvania to await execution.

10 Pacing the cage

My escape ruined any hope I had of ever leaving prison alive (I was now serving a total of 105 years on top of my death sentence) but, strangely enough, for the first time in my life I felt free to be anything I wanted. It simply did not matter any more. I fully expected to die in prison, either by execution or of old age. So, before I left this life, I decided to find out who I was.

The moment I asked my father to call the FBI office in Philadelphia and inform them of my whereabouts, I took my first step towards being 'different'. I cannot fully express what this means in written words, as it is one of those things you just know. It was as if being brought to this point through all the pain and misery of my early life had at last flipped a switch in me marked 'on'. I guess, knowing that my escape attempt had ruined all my chances of appeal and knowing that I was going to remain in prison for the rest of my life, I finally began to live.

It's such a simple thing, yet inside me I really felt as if all of the events I had witnessed and all the hardships I had lived through had brought me to a very momentous point. I was sitting in this hot, nasty-smelling cell on Death Row in FSP Raiford (also known as Starke prison) when that thought came to me. Starke was the main prison where the state of Florida held its Death Row prisoners in the 1980s and I was being held here awaiting my return to Pennsylvania.

I was housed in its old 'East Unit' on Q-Wing, just two flights up from the room that contained the electric chair. Starke made Huntingdon look like a hotel by comparison, with 1,100 men locked up in solitary confinement twenty-three or twenty-four hours a day, versus a mere 145 held on B-Block in Huntingdon.

It would take a few months for the relevant paperwork to come through, so I had no choice but to endure the terrible heat of a Florida summer in this place built on top of an old swamp. Temperatures reached 100 degrees plus and the humidity was as high as ninety per cent. It was so humid and hot in the unit that the nurses dispensed saline tablets in order to prevent men locked up in their cells all day from dying of dehydration.

The 'East Unit' at Starke is the wildest place I have ever spent time in. No matches were allowed in the whole prison as previously inmates had used them to make gunpowder in order to shoot each other with homemade guns. Q-Wing consisted of a single line of five cells with a shower room configured out of the space where Cell 2 would have been, between Cells 1 and 3. I was placed in Cell 3. Each cell had a solid metal door that could be closed across the set of open bars that fronted it. These bars, in which there was another, sliding door also made of bars, were receded two feet into the solid sidewalls. Basically, each cell was a space within a cement block. They were designed so that if the guards closed that outer metal door, you were left inside a concrete hollow enclosure with only a small five-by-five-inch window cut into the door to allow the staff to look in on you. It was impossible for you to harm anyone in one of those security cells and the guards could just drop open a slot in the door and feed you through the hole.

The 'East Unit' was where they held you for your last days alive before they took you downstairs and sat you down in 'Ol' Sparky', as the guards fondly called the electric chair in Florida.

I knew I was not going down there to visit him, so Ol' Sparky held no threat for me. I just had to make it through the gruelling heat before returning to Pennsylvania to fight to have my appeals reinstated. From there I had to find the will to hope for a miracle of some sort.

Sharing Q-Wing with me were: in Cell 1, Ted; in Cell 4, 'Frog'; in Cell 5, James; in Cell 6, Ronnie. When the guards closed the unit door and went downstairs to their 'control area', we were left entirely to ourselves in this strange, secluded world.

All the cells were connected by a ventilation duct which allowed the man in Cell 4 to speak to the guy in Cell 3 on his left by his sink, or he could speak to Cell 5 by leaning down and talking into the metal vent cover located beside his toilet on his right. Also, every cell backed on to the wall of a cell in the wing behind it, so the prisoner in Cell 5 on Q-Wing could also speak to the prisoner in Cell 5 on R-Wing, directly behind him. I was able to talk to Frog in Cell 4, but not to Ted in Cell 1 without having to talk loudly, as we were separated by the shower unit. The truth was that I was glad about this. For Ted was none other than Theodore 'Ted' Bundy, one of the world's most notorious serial killers.

Ted Bundy was also probably the most hated inmate I had ever met. I learned this immediately. As soon as the guards placed me in my cell and left, the other prisoners started to call to me through the vents telling me not to deal with that 'baby-killing scumbag' in Cell 1.

In response to being abused like that, Ted aimed comments back to the others along the line of cells. I had no clue at this stage which prisoner was in which cell; they were all just disembodied voices coming at me through the vents. The other inmates all took it in turns to yell into the vent over the top of Ted, telling me how his boasting had ruined everyone else's prison visits.

Apparently, Ted had managed to get one of his so-called 'Death Row groupie' girlfriends pregnant on a visit. Then 'Big Mouth' Ted had gone and told the press that he was able to have sex in prison. When the prison administration found out, they had taken away contact visits for everyone on Death Row, only allowing the inmates to see their families from behind glass. As a result, everyone on Death Row wanted to kill Ted for taking away their precious ability to hold or touch their families.

I tried to stay out of it. I was going back to Pennsylvania in a short while and all I wanted was just to get out of this place without being killed by one of the other inmates. I made no comments on what was being told to me. Mostly, I just spoke to Frog in the cell next to me, who was also from Philadelphia. In 1985 Florida was still routinely killing inmates and I knew he was facing a date with the electric chair as he was convicted of abducting the owner of a furniture store chain and killing him. Frog was desperate to find a way out. He would be the first of these men I came to know who was put to death. He knew his days were short when we met.

The man in the cell that backed on to mine was named Jesse. To me, he was just a quiet voice through the wall who invited me to play chess. By each numbering our chessboard squares, we could play a game of chess by calling out our moves in turn, as in the children's game Battleship, and placing both sets of pieces accordingly.

Raiford was almost entirely indoors. One of the few times you actually saw another prisoner was when the guards felt like giving you some exercise and placed you in small dog-kennel-like cages located in a yard between two of the buildings.

We barely got any time out there, though; it was just too hot outside and they did not make any real effort to let us out anyway. From my wing of Q-Block, only James went out regularly into the heat.

That meant that the only other time you saw another inmate was when you signed up for the 'law library'. Each man was entitled to have six hours per week in the library, where a small number of law books were kept on hand.

The library, which consisted of a pair of cages situated in a large room next to the prison's main corridor, was located just beside the entrance to Q-Wing. We were taken there two at a time and placed in a separate cage each before our handcuffs were removed through a small slot cut into the cage door. When we went to the library we sat on white plastic chairs in our individual cages reading law journals or books, trying to find legal arguments with which to fight our cases.

I signed up for the law library every chance I got as I intended to go back to Pennsylvania and fight, no matter what. Now that I had made the choice to give myself up and face the battle, I knew I needed all the legal weapons I could muster. It seemed to everyone else that I was completely screwed legally at this point, but all I wanted was for the truth to be told, even if I died in the process. Therefore, I really needed to try and learn the law in order to become proficient in presenting my appeal arguments.

In Joe Bullen I had a lawyer who had already made it clear he thought I was guilty, so I had little to lose there. And I had no money to employ another lawyer. So I had better get sharp and become my own champion. It was only the thought that my family knew I was actually innocent that kept me going, and I owed it to them to try. I figured that if I had the nerve to hand myself over to police, then I was also brave enough to find out what I was about as a person.

That was all I thought about every day. In fact, that was what I was thinking about when I was brought into the library one day, only to find that I was going to have to share my time there with Ted. Now, he and I had already had a few cold exchanges during one of the air-vent conversations. Although he had not aimed his sharp-tongued wit directly at me, I had bristled when he had started butting in on one of my conversations. Whenever any of his enemies spoke, Ted gave a sarcastic running commentary and made barbed jokes about their moronic levels of speaking. Any and every conversation that I or anyone else had he regarded as his chance to get back at his many tormentors.

Over the past weeks Ted had listened to me tell Frog through the vents that I was going to be extradited back to Pennsylvania. I did not realise it immediately, but Ted had deliberately chosen to come out to the library with me that day. We were going to be left there for two hours by ourselves and during that time, he decided, he would dazzle me with his amazing command of law (he had studied law at university) and show me how I could thwart the extradition order back to Pennsylvania. I had gotten my legal papers out of their manila envelope and was just settling down to read a law book when he started on this terribly rehearsed introduction to his 'show'.

Standing there in his blue denim trainers and orange jumpsuit, with his prison number printed on its left breast pocket, he looked like just another middle-aged prisoner. Then he adapted this 'position', in which he perched on his left leg while resting his right leg on the seat of the plastic chair. Then, as he leaned back as far away from me as he could, he tried to give the air of being 'composed'.

I just looked at him, curious to see how he was going to play me. Everyone in the entire prison knew his story: over a four-year period from 1974 to 1978 he had raped and murdered at least twenty-nine women, most of them college girls.

I also knew that this man was really bright and dangerous but, having had to kind of grow up in the harsh environment of Huntingdon prison, I was hard to impress.

Ted began: 'Ya know, I've been extradited twice and I know every flaw in the Interstate Compact Agreement, so I'm telling you right now, you can cheat Pennsylvania out of bringing you back to fry you until *after* you've served your sentences in Florida.'

He said this as if he were trying to sell a hopeless man new hope. But it was a pure 'lawyer' move, done with the smarminess of a pro trying to persuade you that he was your new guy, with you all the way.

But before he could get going properly, I took the smirk right off of his face by cutting in brutally with: 'I actually asked to go back to Pennsylvania, Ted. I'm not like you; I don't get my rocks off murdering little girls while thinking I am killing my bad "mommy" who was mean to me.' I said all this in a mocking tone, adding the last bit in a child-like sing-song voice.

He went nuts. In a flash, this cord of a vein throbbed in his forehead and then the jugular vein in his neck became mottled and swollen as it pulsed away. It was frightening to see this otherwise apparently quiet person fly into such a rage so fast. I barely had time to hold the manila folder up in front of me before the first mouthful of spittle splattered all over my glasses. He was literally frothing at the mouth as he screeched out endless threats and screamed filthy, degrading things about my mother.

It was so scary that I kind of laughed nervously – although I had certainly set out to annoy, I had not really thought that what I said would provoke this sort of reaction. I was staring in the face of a creature on fire with rage.

I ducked behind my folder and waited as the sound of rattling keys and hurried footsteps running down the long corridor outside indicated some guards were on their way to see what was going on.

I was taking shots at him verbally here and there, but I was stunned by the sheer rage and demented explosiveness of this person. Ted Bundy was a very slender man – no more than 160 pounds on his best day – and I was physically much bigger than him at 6 feet 2 inches tall and weighing over 200 pounds. Also I could handle myself, I felt. But as he kicked and smashed his fists against the metal cage bars between us and spewed out all that madness, I really was not sure. It was one of the creepiest experiences of my life. Just to witness such a complete change in a human being to the point that his voice changed. He even smelled different. I really mean it: he exuded this terrible odour of ammonia. It was as if I had just stepped on some hidden mine within his personality.

It took the guards about twenty minutes to go and get some shields and two sets of handcuffs in order to take both Ted and me out of there. During that whole time he continued to kick, trying to destroy the barrier between us, and scream and spit at me. Having his saliva on my face and in my hair truly sickened me. He thoroughly scared me because here I was standing next to something so evil that it was not human.

I admit that there were times in the days that followed when I wished that, as well as being taken out of that law library following our encounter, I had been taken straight back to Huntingdon. For the rest of my days at Raiford, this madman became the bane of my existence. Every morning he started on me and kept at it all day long. No matter what I was doing, he did what he could to get back at me.

I tried every approach in dealing with him. Perhaps unwisely, I taunted him by telling the others all about our encounter and what I had said about him killing his mom. I tried to drown him out with noise. I tried to block him out by playing chess for hours and hours with Jesse. It did not matter. He met every challenge and he tormented me every day because he knew that, sooner or later, I would be leaving so there would be no comeback.

It hurt. If only I had kept my mouth shut and played along with him, none of this would have happened. Once, a particularly slow guard accidentally gave him my mail, so I had to put up with him reading my parents' letter to me out loud over and over, claiming that he was masturbating over it as well. I really was not happy when that happened.

In order to get away from Ted, I tried to go outside into the exercise yard as much as possible. It was only James and I who could put up with the intense heat and humidity of the yard. Ronnie was too fat to make it down the steps, so he just stayed inside all the time. Jesse did come out, but his wing used a set of cages a bit away from ours.

So, I sweated my ass off out there, the only place I could get away from my tormentor. Just me and James, who was this little 5 foot 2 inch, 110 lb black guy from Cell 5, doing his endless push-ups and sit-ups. Trying to escape the madness inside by roasting in the heat, I guessed.

I sat in the strip of shade cast by the fence, trying not to get burned badly during my one hour out in the sunlight. Even so, I always got a headache and felt dizzy out there. Meanwhile, James did nothing but work out. He kept trying to get me to join him in his cage so that we could work out together. A bit of me wanted to, but something in me never let its guard down. Just as well.

In one of our last conversations out there in those cages, once everyone knew I was being shipped back, James told me that he had killed seven human beings. I would have been number eight if he had had his chance. He told me that as well. No emotion, just told me right out.

James had been on Death Row once before in Florida, in the 1970s, but had been spared execution as there had been a change in the law and his sentence had been commuted to life imprisonment. When they reinstated a new death penalty law a few years later, he began killing inmates. He told me that he just wanted to be killed, as they had promised would happen to him years before. So he decided to kill an inmate in the chapel during Mass in front of thirty witnesses. 'It gave me back my chance to be executed,' he said between incessant push-ups. However, the state failed to put him back on Death Row for that, so he went on to kill another two inmates before they finally granted him his wish. He wanted to die, and so he decided that the state was going to do it for him.

Frog had warned me to stay clear of this guy previously, but he was such a slight man that it was difficult to feel afraid of him. Also, he spoke in this strange little croaking voice, because at one point he had been strangled so badly that all his vocal cords had been deadened. I found myself having to lean over to hear him speak, even when there was only the two of us out in the yard.

Although I knew James was trying to get me to let my guard down (though I never knew why), he was so physically unthreatening that I was kind of lulled into a false sense of security with him. Foolishly, I probably would have let my guard down at some point and gone into the cage with him.

That is, if it were not for the fact that finally, after months of waiting, the extradition papers came through and I was told that I was being brought back to Pennsylvania to face my charges there. Just like that, I was leaving.

At last I could get away from the remorseless heat and daily torments inside of that little pocket of misery on earth called 'Q-Wing'.

My parting gift from James on one of the last days when we were out in the cages together was simply this: he told me that, not only had he killed those seven people and murdered those other inmates to get himself put back on Death Row, he had done it because they were white.

He looked me right in the face and said calmly, 'If I had got a shot, I *was* gonna kill you.' Then added, 'It ain't nothing personal as you's a pretty cool white boy'n'all, but I'm gonna kill me as many of yous devils as I can before they take me out.'

Then he simply went back to doing his sit-ups in the corner of his cage like it was no different from him sharing his favourite childhood memory with me. As freakishly scary as Ted Bundy was, it was this man with his icily calm demeanour who chilled me more. Looking at James's face was like looking into the eyes of a great white shark. There was no soul behind them; he did not even need the spark of anger to find his hate, he was well beyond that.

As I stood two feet away from James, talking through the fence to him and watching him pace the cage even as we spoke, I understood that it was not anger or misery that drove him to keep moving; it was this quiet resolution simply to kill every white person who came near him until 'they' killed him. To this day, every time I hear the Bruce Cockburn song 'Pacing the Cage' I get chills down my spine thinking about how James's words stilled my heart that day. To him, it was the ultimate sign of respect actually to tell me that he would have killed me had he been given the chance.

It was as if he saw me as a trophy he had earned the right to nurture before adding to his collection. I swear to God, he was the scariest person I have ever met.

11 'Welcome back from vacation, Mr Yarris'

On 21 October 1985, the Florida authorities released me into the care of six armed deputies from Delaware and Chester Counties, Pennsylvania, who had driven down to Florida in three cars to get me. They brought with them a sub-machine gun, as well as 10 lbs of chains, handcuffs and leg irons, just to make sure I was coming back this time. We were going to drive the 1,100 miles from Raiford prison back to Pennsylvania in a convoy shadowed by state police at each border between Florida and Pennsylvania, with me in the middle car. We would be driving at 100 miles per hour the whole way. You can do the math: even driving flat out, it would take eleven hours at a minimum to cover that distance. Oh and no, we were not stopping for me to use the bathroom again on the way back!

I witnessed one of the most beautiful sunsets in my life as I rode along US route I-95 north through North Carolina that fall. I was turned sideways in the rear seat of the sheriff's car, craning my neck to see this blood-red glow in the sky mix with a golden and silver shade all laced in front of the blue-black colour that was being brought on by nightfall.

I knew I was going back to Huntingdon prison, where I was not going to have a window in my cell for a very long time, so I was trying to soak in every moment of that sunset. I also realised that I was going back to hell. I had a kind of sick feeling inside of me knowing that I would not be very popular with the Huntingdon staff after my escape. I knew there had been a newspaper article written about it that had highlighted the lack of security at Huntingdon. In it, the journalist had torn into the guards who had searched me before I left for court on the day of my escape. They had obviously not searched me properly, he said. How could I have taken off my handcuffs during the escape if I did not have a handcuff key on me before I left the prison?

Two guards had been sent home for a week without pay, thanks to this article. It didn't take a lot to see that I was going to pay for that, as well as be used as an example to others to discourage them from trying to run.

Yet the one thing that still bothered me more than any of this, and gave me bad dreams for months, was James, my fellow inmate at Starke prison. As far as he was concerned, I had just been 'prey'. What haunted me were his eyes and how he kept looking at me as he bobbed back and forth in his cage, his body swaying in the opposite direction to his head. Always moving. Always looking at me with those unflinching, dead eyes.

Returning to Huntingdon was not quite as I expected, actually. When I got there, I was placed in a cell separated from the rest of Death Row and left by myself for months. I was not allowed to exercise with the other Death Row men and I was kept away from them as much as possible by the staff, who wanted to quell any desire I might inspire in others to escape.

There were also a few whispers to me on the way to the yard or showers from the guards that 'It won't be long now, Yarris' – meaning that I had a beating coming to me and they wanted me to know it.

Even so, it was better to be on the guards' 'attack list' than be stalked by some sociopath like James, as you only expected a certain level of violence from guards. Still, their taunts and threats unnerved me. I knew it was all having an effect on me. I began losing all of my hair. I lost weight. I had to undergo extensive dental surgery and it seemed as if I was always ill. It is truly hard to deal with battling constantly on two fronts: my legal struggle and my environment. I was happy to be lost in law books and prepare briefs for myself and anyone else who needed them, as they stopped me reminding myself all the time that it was me and my big mouth that had put me in here on Death Row twice now.

The press had not reported that I had turned myself in to the FBI, so at least I was spared the scorn of the other inmates. For, if it had become widely known that I had turned myself in, then to them it would have seemed that I was too weak to run and this was where I belonged. Not a single person would have believed that I had come back because I wanted to prove that I wasn't guilty. So, I just let the authorities have their 'spin' in the press of my being recaptured in a car while I slept, and the other inmates seemed none the wiser.

I was much more worried about what I was going to be subjected to for having escaped. Let's face it: this was Huntingdon, where they send you to be broken. No one either knew or cared if I was innocent; as to them I was just a sick-minded lunatic. I was also an escapee. I knew that my ordeal was far from over, but the extra cruelty lay in how long I had to wait for it to happen.

Some guards who had been suspended for not searching me properly came by to tell me how I had cost them a week's pay. They did not threaten me overtly. They did not have to. It was widely acknowledged that at some point I was going to have their lost wage packet taken out on my flesh, and they did not have to lift a finger to get it done. They had come to see me before their revenge was taken, and they would come back to laugh afterwards. There was nothing unusual or sinister about this, it was just Huntingdon rules.

On and on the time dragged as my first days turned into weeks and nothing happened. I never let my guard down and it ate into me, but eventually I settled back into the prison routine and they put me back in Cell 443 on B-Block.

I tried to ignore everything that was going on around me and to focus my mindset in a different direction. Outside of my cell the entire prison population doubled overnight and the once-hushed world of Huntingdon became a rampant madhouse. The USA had emptied its mental wards in the mid 1980s at about the same time that the crack epidemic hit the country and suddenly the prison population rose from roughly one million to two million people.

This all had a direct impact on Death Row in Huntingdon, as it was housed in a block within the main prison. Although in 1986 and 1987 there were only fifty or so men on Death Row in B-Block, there was still room for about ninety more prisoners in the disciplinary housing cells built behind ours. Imagine ninety men with varying degrees of mental health problems being locked in cells twenty-three hours a day with no structure. Soon those cells were being filled with former mental patients who were not capable of participating in normal prison activities.

They were also often being preyed on by the young drug gangs who, thanks to the crack epidemic, were pouring into prison at that time. Thrown into solitary confinement cells on B-Block behind the Death Row inmates, they caused mayhem on the unit.

All day and all night there were men yelling and banging and cursing and worse. There were inmates standing at their doors urinating and throwing faeces on the staff or other inmates. It was as if a switch had been flipped and the authorities could no longer control anything. The guards would be beating people all day long if they tried to enforce the 'no talking' rule upon so many men who were suffering from such obvious mental disorders.

The entire dynamics of the prison were changing. No longer did I stand out as a young man; now it was full of men in their twenties like me. However, this new world of mayhem created outside my cell made it easy for me to be forgotten for a while as other men did crazy things like jump to their deaths or set fire to themselves. Many times have I heard the wet smack as someone's body hit the floor from forty feet up; I also vividly recall an inmate burning himself alive while screaming out that God was a lie and he was going to prove it.

The one thing that saved me from this cacophony was my first set of stereo headphones. Before, the rule had been that you could only cover one ear or listen softly to a radio in your cell. As soon as they changed the rule I desperately sought out the best headphones I could get. My mother bought me a pair for my birthday and I wore them constantly from morning until night. Then, with my new stereo ear buds cutting off all external sound, I just retreated into a blissfully different world created by the music on the radio – NPR or BBC World Service. As soon as I got out of bed, I put on my headphones.

When I went to sleep I plugged my ears with these homemade earplugs I had modelled out of little plastic bags stuffed with balls of wet toilet tissue and sealed with a match. It was the only way I could get to sleep.

And with all that confusion going on outside the four walls of my cell, extraordinarily enough, I began to flourish. I used being in solitary confinement to my advantage in that it gave me the time to educate myself. I spent hours each day reading until eventually, having taught myself for years, I moved on to do a college correspondence course in psychology and human development. I ploughed through thousands of books and in so doing managed to change my cell from the framework of a bleak and empty existence into the foundation of my growth. It was always such a short step from trying to rise above the evil in such a place to just leaping to one's death there. Either I learned how to grow up or I died.

I worked my way from just learning to read to really becoming accomplished in writing legal argument and studying serology (the study of blood serum) and other fields of science related to my case. I made a pact with three other men that we would send off fifteen used books a week to a very kind bookstore near State College, Pennsylvania, which would send us back ten different ones. I sought out all sorts of things to learn and study until I hit upon the idea of trading my legal skills for things like pre-paid envelopes.

There were two forms of currency on B-Block: envelopes and cigarettes. The men who smoked sought out the cigarettes; the ones who wanted to communicate with the outside world sought out the envelopes. Writing letters, or 'doing your bit' as we called it, to stay connected to the world was hugely valued as it was our one line of communication to our families.

I began to barter with some of the non-Death Row men on B-Block for envelopes in return for me taking exams or getting college credits for them. You see, if you wanted to impress the parole board with how hard you had worked in prison you took courses in psychology or human development. I took exams, I wrote theses and I offered legal help to those who needed it in exchange for envelopes.

My parents were not able to send me much, so I had to rely on my own resources to help prove my innocence. I wrote endless letters to officials and I hounded reporters for help. I was turned down by every human rights group in the country at the time, though I cannot say I blame them. It's hard to convince people that you are innocent when you have escaped from Death Row.

I was so immersed in my world of college courses, briefs and every kind of novel I could get my hands on that, in the blink of an eye, 1985 turned into 1987.

Then, one night in June 1987, at about 8.30 p.m., I was taken from my cell by two guards who did not normally work on Death Row. They told me I was being taken to 'use the property room'. This was the place where inmates' belongings are kept, in another building connected to the rear of B-Block. In it were boxes filled with excess cell property and once every ninety days a prisoner on Death Row could ask to swap excess legal materials or books in his cell for those in his boxes in the property room. Every Death Row prisoner was allowed only two paper sacks of legal work and one paper sack of toiletries and/or underclothes in his cell at one time. Cardboard was considered too dangerous as it could be rolled into deadly 'spears' with which men could try and stab staff.

No big deal, I thought, when I did not recognise the guards; there were so many new ones working here now. I thought nothing of it as we walked the forty or so yards from my cell around the corner of B-Block and into the outer doors of the property-room building. It was only as we were walking up the stairs to the second floor and I saw there was a light on in the big room that I knew my time had come.

Both guards had manoeuvred behind me, not one in front and one in back of me as protocol mandated. I was afraid they were going to kick me or tear into my legs from behind with clubs. Then, just as I turned the corner into the property room on the second floor, I came face-to-face with four guards holding riot batons – three-foot-long clubs made from solid oak. The guards had leather gloves on and wore surgical masks to protect them from the blood splatters. I never said a word and nor did they as they laid into me. We all knew what this was about. I was praying I'd be knocked out in the first blows, so I would be spared being conscious through the entire attack. You always try to rush at them and make them go for your head as it means that at least you don't suffer when they hit your legs and butt with those clubs. I know it is an insane logic, but I was fully aware of what they did to escapees. I knew I was about to have the piss literally beaten out of me.

The purpose of bringing me up to the second floor was so that those inmates on Death Row whose cells were on a level with the property room could see what they were doing to me through the windows of B-Block. With the lights on inside the property room and the inmates on my unit aware that someone had just been taken out of his cell, the significance of the event was not lost on them.

I had been taken there not only as punishment for what I had done, but as an example to others. I left a piece of my eye on the floor of that room that evening and some of my fellow prisoners told me later that the beating went on for a good two to three minutes. I woke up in the disciplinary cells with a detached retina in my left eye and my legs looking like a series of railroad ties, with marks tattooed across the sides and backs of my thighs. It hurt to stand, and it was agony to lie down on the plastic-covered mattress. I peed blood and I cried and I slowly healed and I swore revenge and I seethed and I was hurt and yet I felt completely impotent to do a damn thing. In time I just hid behind my prison-issue eyeglasses and quietly read and listened to music in order to drown out this madness while I waited for a miracle, or for time itself to run out.

I never got anyone back for the attack; I never stabbed or assaulted any member of staff. I took my beating and hoped that was the end of it.

I know it seems crazy, but in time what the guards did to me started to make me want to be 'different' from them, even more than from the other prisoners. I was sick of all these macho guards hurting people, instead of just doing their jobs like the majority of the staff. I was sick of this tiresome world of 'inmate pecking orders' and petty, stupid criminals. I did not want to be accepted by the men on Death Row, but nor did I want to deal with the staff either. Weirdly enough, I enjoyed being ostracised by other inmates. I just kept to a small band of guys near me who were not caught up in the hierarchical struggles of the Death Row tough guys. Luckily, they seemed not to care who was loudest or baddest.

The days once again blended into that endless passage of time you only find in solitary confinement. I didn't go to the exercise yard for months; I also bathed in my cell instead of going to the showers.

I just kept to myself. Despite the permanent damage to my left eye, the beating in the property room didn't really bother me mentally. It was a relief, actually. Anyone who held a grudge against me had been paid in full and it was widely known what I had been attacked for.

Afterwards I was more or less left alone again as more high-profile criminals were sent to Death Row for them to bang heads with. The sad thing is, the murder rate was the number one issue in the presidential election campaigns of 1984 and there were 2,500 murders a year in the US. I was on Death Row at a time when your average 'garden variety' murder was being topped by ever more heinous crimes. I sat there with men who had killed as many as thirteen human beings, or who had stuck guns to children's heads in order to rob innocent people before later murdering those children's fathers so as to get away with it.

As I sat there inside Cell 443 being quietly forgotten, I didn't really know what I was waiting for. Although my right to appeal against the murder conviction had been reinstated following my return to custody, it was hardly surprising that, whatever errors or evidence abuse had been made during my trial, the State Supreme Court was not going to overturn my conviction and order a new trial. No case on record has ever been reversed following the escape of the prisoner. And the fact that I was a Death Row prisoner at the time of my escape was an additional aggravator. My attorney, Joe Bullen, would file my appeal, but it was duty and law, not conviction and hope, that made him do so. I was just left to my books and my headphones, and the pictures of family on the walls of my cell built up as I dived head-on into finding out just who the hell I was.

That's what I did, I guess. I sat there and asked myself who I was, and then I decided to find out through the oddly helpful gift that having an addictive personality bestows:

I got sucked completely into the world of literature and the minds of the writers who created some of the world's greatest works – authors like Dumas, or Hugo or Trevanian. Thanks to my music and my books, I left that cell on a daily basis through the creativity of others and travelled as far away as I could.

I also spent my days learning the most intricate or empowering words I could, especially if they were relevant to my situation. From this was born my fascination with 'triskaidekaphobia' (the fear of thirteen) because I always seemed to have bad things happen to me on the 13th. That was the first word I really wanted to understand.

As well as novels, I started to read the biographies of my favourite writers. I loved to find out more about the people who had written those books and I wanted to know how they could write something that struck me as being so wonderful or showing me a better view of the world. I was searching for that one thing that impelled each writer to turn life's many painful moments into a creative outpouring that could be embraced by people who never even knew them.

I am not being coy. I really was fascinated by the ability of the human mind to turn life's journey into compelling stories. In all those books I learned so many simple truths about how we keep repeating our lives in so many similar ways. They also finally offered me a reprieve from being eaten alive by the memories that could have meant my life had ended at the age of twenty.

12 'What is life outside like today?'

All throughout 1986 and 1987 I was living on my own 'schedule'. I was sleeping in the afternoons, waking in the early evening and then, just when most of the heavily medicated inmates were easing back a bit on their madness, I would stay up late at night, writing legal work and taking psychology correspondence courses.

In solitary confinement on Death Row, as long as you ate and your cell was not overflowing with newspapers and garbage, the staff were happy to let you do whatever you wanted. The lights inside the cell were in your own control, so if you wanted to sit and watch television twenty-four hours a day until your brain turned to mush, fine. If you wanted to read or exercise all day and all night, fine. As long as you 'showed some movement' for the head count three times a day, did not harm yourself or assault others in the showers, and did not cause problems while going out to the cages for exercise, you were left alone.

Late one afternoon in the early part of December 1987 I was woken by a guard, who informed me that I had a visitor. My parents' annual Christmas visit was only a week away, so I wasn't sure who this could be who had come to see me. I had no other regular visitors; in fact, I rarely had visitors at all and, frankly, that was OK with me.

It takes a lot of emotional effort to go into a room, face people and put on a show. Especially when it's your family you must face. On this occasion I was still groggy from having been in a deep sleep as I went through the ritual of being 'dressed out' – that is, strip searched – by the guards before leaving my cell for the visit. Once I was dressed again, the guards took me out to one of the attorney visiting rooms, right beside B-Block, that were used for all Death Row prisoners' visits.

I was told to sit down on the chair bolted to the floor of the prisoners' side of the visiting room while the guards stood in front of me dealing with my handcuffs. As soon as they stepped away, I looked up and smiled. It was Pam. Pam Tucker was the woman who headed up the western Pennsylvania abolitionist movement in 1987. The mother of two girls, who were the centre of her world, she split her life between looking after her family and fighting for the humane treatment of men waiting to die – and I admired her for that.

I was glad there were people like Pam in the world, who really cared about those the state was going to kill, and treated us as human beings. She was one of the very few people I wrote to at that time. I liked her character too – she had a good sense of humour, which she certainly needed fighting the death penalty at a time when the streets of America were becoming bloodier by the day.

Sitting there to Pam's left and just watching as she and I chatted easily to each other was another woman. Very well dressed, thirtyish and with blonde hair, she just smiled at me as I sat there smiling back at them both. Pam introduced her as a friend of hers from Pittsburgh who had come with her that day to talk to five men and find out what the treatment and conditions were like here at Huntingdon. She was then going to write a report they would be presenting to the Commissioner of Corrections.

The other woman said her name was Jacqueline, but her friends called her Jacque and she had only just joined the abolitionist movement. She said she wanted to thank me for taking the time to talk to them as part of their effort to improve conditions. Pam had asked her to compile the report as she had experience of dealing with state procedures in her role as a union representative in the hospital in which she had worked as a psychiatric aide for six years. Having heard what the other four men had to say, she continued, she was determined to help us. Death Row prisoners should, at the very least, be housed separately from the general prison population and not mixed up with men who had been placed there for punishment.

I was still a bit subdued from having recently rejoined the wakened world, so I just hid behind my big plastic prison-issue eyeglasses and watched her every facial expression. When she had finished this very sincere outpouring of why she was there and what she had decided to talk to me about today, I made a small joke about how I wished I could drink real coffee for once in my life, that's the one condition I'd love to see changed around here!

Pam laughed at the insider joke. Prison coffee has a unique flavour that you have to taste to understand what I mean. It is a cheap mix of coffee, chicory and 'additives' boiled up in huge vats in burlap bags the size of bed pillows. These are then cooked for hours in order to provide for a prison population of 2,300. In prison they call coffee 'mud' for good reason. Let a cup of prison coffee sit for a while, pour off the excess fluid, look into the bottom of the cup and you will see a fine layer of 'mud' – the residue of boiled burlap and other cost-saving ingredients.

As Pam and I fell into similar exchanges, I noticed out of the corner of my eye that Jacque was watching me intently.

It was as if she were not familiar with this sort of two-way conversation with a prisoner, instead of the usual recitation of a long list of grievances against the system or tales of his mistreatment. And the more I ignored the reason why these two women were there but instead asked about life in the outside world and anything else I could come up with, the more it must have occurred to Jacque that I was not bothered by my situation. She saw that it was natural for me to come there and just be 'Nicky', a guy who acted for all the world as if it were normal for him to be sitting there chatting with two women.

I can only guess at what the other men had talked to them about before I got there, as they seemed really shell-shocked at the depravity and levels of violence perpetrated in Huntingdon on a daily basis by inmates and staff alike. Pam worked into the conversation some mention of what they had already been told, but I was not really game for that, so I deflected the conversation elsewhere. I was just enjoying the moment. Having spent months in a hermit-like existence, staying up all night and not venturing out even into the exercise yard, I wanted to appreciate all the very fine nuances of our conversation, just talking and laughing. Eventually the obvious became too much for Jacque and she asked me pointedly, 'Why doesn't all of this bother you?'

I wanted to say so many complicated things in reply to that simple question. I wanted to show this person that I had my own reasons for wanting to be different from everyone else here. And I certainly did not want to be seen as one of those inmates who have been so conditioned by prison that they have given up the struggle. But I had no clue how to say it all.

I was just flooded with shame. Either I could humiliate myself by saying that I was not guilty but I was here on Death Row because of my own stupid mouth – in which case I would have had to launch into the entire saga of how I had made up the ridiculous story that had landed me here – or I could let her think that I was a murderer who deserved to be here. While I was not keen to have anyone think that I was at ease here because I was a psychotic murderer, nor did I have the will to make the huge effort it would take to convince them of the contrary.

As I sat there looking at this well-groomed woman who had no clue who I was before that moment, I was so aware that, although I could not care less how the prison staff interpreted my lack of concern for my living conditions (since they all thought I was guilty anyway), it was much harder to explain to someone from outside these walls that I was this way because I just chose to be.

So, I swallowed my heart in my throat twice before I came out with the only response I could think of: 'I'm sure Pam can fill you in on my case on the way home. It's a real twisted story that makes you proud to be American.'

It was hard to tell, but my answer seemed to play on Jacque's patience. She was not impolite but she did not enquire further. I went through the rest of the visit knowing that there was an unmentioned 300lb gorilla seated next to me and for the entire remainder of the time we all conspired to dance artfully around it.

I went back to my cell and replayed to myself every detail of every second of my time in that visiting room. Years of being tormented by the memories of my past life playing out endlessly in my head had left me with a finely honed ability to play over and over any new encounters. I re-listened to every word that I could recall speaking to both Pam and Jacque. I rose through the sweet exchanges and died inside again and again as I dwelt upon how I had failed to defend myself. I looked again at every detail of the clothes

Jacque wore and every strand of her hair. At will, I saw again every movement that she made.

It was both sweet and painful to sift through every little thing that had resulted from Jacque and Pam coming to pull me out of that 'nothingness' of spending endless days locked up by myself in a concrete box.

Exactly one week after my visit from Pam and Jacque I was awakened once more in the middle of the afternoon to be told that I had a visitor. This was an obvious cause for alarm, as two visits in the span of a week meant only one thing: bad news.

As I entered the attorney visiting room once again to sit down on the bolted-down inmate chair, and again had my handcuffs placed in front of me by the guards, I looked up and saw Jacque, alone. She was pacing back and forth nervously on the other side of the room barrier, impatient for the guards to leave us. Then, as soon as the snap of the lock had sounded our being alone, we both spoke at once. I asked her why she was there. Had she gotten lost? I joked. I had never thought I would see either Jacque or Pam again.

Jacque looked at me and replied earnestly: 'During the three-hour drive home from here with Pam last week, I kept trying to steer the conversation back to you. I found myself asking her about you; not about your case and what put you here – I know you invited me to get that from her and I did a bit – but what I really wanted to know was why you are the way you seem.' And then finally, while standing awkwardly between the two wooden visiting chairs on the other side of this tiny room, she said simply, 'I cannot stop thinking about *you*.'

As she spoke I looked at myself in the reflection created by her dark jacket's shadow on the glass barrier between us. I saw my thinning hair, which had left me nearly bald across my forehead; I saw my thick plastic-framed eyeglasses; and I saw my skin bleached white by six years of having been locked away in a windowless cell. What could anyone see in me? My face was drawn and haggard from losing some teeth and I had not shaved since the last 'shower day', three days previously. I felt as unattractive and inhuman as it was possible to feel in front of a member of the opposite sex.

And I was so caught up in how I looked right then that I thought she could not really be speaking about that person I saw there every day in the closest I ever normally came to a mirror – the sheet of metal bolted to the wall above my rusted-out toilet. Even without a proper mirror, I knew from the many taunts of both inmates and guards that I looked how I felt.

When she stopped talking I was trapped in that moment when you know your thoughts are written all over your face but you are at a loss as to what to do. I understood perfectly well what she had said and it stole all my courage. I started being facetious, but she was not smiling along with me and all my efforts were just so out of tune with her. I knew it and she knew it.

I sat still and brimmed with tears as I looked down at my thin, ill-fitting blue canvas prison-issue prison shoes. I hated it. I truly hated how much my ordeal had left me looking like some mental misfit who was rotting away here in hell waiting to be killed.

I was starting to get angry, so she spoke to me in this soothing way, which I interpreted as condescension and made me further angered. She saw I was getting upset and began to tell me that she did not mean to make me feel bad by not laughing heartily at my jokes. She said that she was just trying to tell me in all sincerity that I had her respect for having displayed such a calm, strong and easy manner in her previous visit. That she felt it was a quality that showed to her that I was not totally lost to whatever had put me there. That, despite what Pam told her had been done to me physically inside prison, I had managed to keep my sense of humour. She admired me for this and she hoped I would keep my sweet outlook.

I really started to feel stupid at this point as I began to think that any 'attraction' she might have felt for me was all imagined on my part.

Here was this person come to offer me moral support for my efforts to deal with the inhumane conditions in prison and I had gotten it all wrong in my lonely little mind. I was bouncing off the mental walls inside of my head as I lost all confidence in my ability to handle the situation. Jacque was not what I had expected and she had not said what I expected. But, having been convicted of being a sexual deviant, I was too churned up with the emotion of trying to deal with a woman to react appropriately. This was just my conditioned response to the way other females treated me regularly in prison and it cut deeply every time. At that moment I sincerely wished she had left me alone and picked out one of the other guys from last week.

When I looked up again, though, I realised that she was not speaking softly any more and slowly we smiled at each other. I did not want to smile too widely as I was missing my front teeth, so I lamely tried to cover my mouth by holding my lips tightly over my gums. I even hated her for looking at me, it hurt so much to think what I must seem like to a woman. The more I tried, and failed, to rebound from all the awkward and difficult feelings I had felt earlier, the more I just wanted to find a graceful way out of here and go back to my cell.

I don't really know how, but eventually we got through those first twenty minutes and then, suddenly, we started talking about how she had studied psychiatry and how she worked with all sorts of mentally impaired children and adults. She started telling me that, as a trained psychiatric aide, she saw at first-hand how much change was needed in the mental health system. She was really frustrated that the insurance companies had found 'treasure' by getting mental patients released into family care so that they were covered by the family's medical insurance and then, once they were inevitably brought back for hospitalisation, the insurance companies could get paid by the state for looking after them.

In response, I told Jacque what a nightmare it was to be housed in prison with all these men who suffered from all sorts of mental disorders. How, if they were not being preyed on by inmates in the general population, they were being thrown into solitary confinement on Death Row. I tried to be as gentle as I could as I told her about how these men were also subject to abuse from the guards, who had not been properly trained to deal with them. It is very hard to watch a supporter of the system be hit forcibly by the real horror of what happens in prison to men trapped by mental illness; also, what it makes the ones who are not disabled do to those who are impaired, simply because these men are so easily exploitable. Most sex-abuse victims in prison are mentally impaired.

Hours passed as we talked about the empowerment and understanding we had both gotten from studying the human mind and child development. Jacque never tried to call for any other inmates to be brought out and, as for me, I just wanted to stay and talk for as long as I could with this real-life human being who really seemed to care.

Every week for the next four months, Jacque drove 225 miles along gruelling mountain roads from Pittsburgh to Huntingdon to visit me and every week we found new things to talk about. I saw in her so many fine qualities and I was enchanted by her sense of humour, as well as how she obviously really cared about people. But what impressed me most about her was how she wanted to make things better for people caught in the system, including men who were just waiting to die.

I also definitely made an impression on her with my efforts to learn as much as I could about humanity and about life once I had lost my right to either of these through my own folly.

I knew that Jacque's visits were becoming really important to me, and as each week passed I grew closer and closer to her. I tried to comb my thinning hair and make myself presentable for her, even though my only sartorial choice was a bright orange jumpsuit. I felt so happy each time she came to see me and so terribly lonely when she left. I found myself writing her ten-page letters following up on all the things we had failed to discuss completely on her visits. I was aware that I had feelings for her that were deepening daily.

I was also absolutely aware that there were men in hopeless situations like mine who simply used women. I did not want to be one of those guys, putting their partner through years of hell in the hope that someday they would 'come home'. I did not have a great past history when it came to honourable behaviour, but now that I was in the process of finding my moral compass I did not want to let anyone down any more than I had previously. I already lived with that terrible feeling that my family was being sucked dry in slow agony as they fought for me. I was aware that there was this terrific pull within me to have someone come here and care for me. But I also knew that there was not likely to be any 'happy ever after' ending. I could not be so cruel to someone who was herself so genuine. I could not be so selfish, even though I knew we were falling deeply in love.

I had no clue how to fight this battle raging within me. But, as I hoped for the best and feared for the worst, I knew that I was going to take the coward's way through all this and let her decide for us. The emotional journey we had embarked on had become such a challenge to me on so many levels. I was not really sure why, but I felt as if I were destined always to learn each lesson in my life only through very meaningful events. Why else was I so aware of these things that none of the other inmates seemed troubled by as they blindly scratched and fought their way through their day-to-day lives?

13 'If I can get science to speak for me, will they listen to science?'

In 1987 Florida became the first state in the USA to convict offenders using evidence based on DNA testing. By the time I read about DNA fingerprinting, as it was first called, in February 1988, this was a science that was being spoken about loudly in another way: 'exoneration'. For, overshadowing any conviction gained in court using this new science was the terrible realisation that the system had 'gotten it wrong' in some very highly publicised cases.

People sentenced to as much as 300 years' imprisonment for a series of rapes were being proven innocent. The whole judicial system was being shaken to its very core. This 'bolt of truth' that DNA testing had suddenly become began opening long-locked doors and setting the innocent free like never before.

In March 1988 I became the first Death Row prisoner in the United States to be granted a request for DNA testing. But how can I express to you what it was then like for me to watch 111 other men be exonerated from

Death Row as I embarked on my mission to prove my innocence?

I was sitting at my desk in Cell 443 on B-Block on 20 February 1988 when I read it. I will always remember that date. Another inmate was about to throw away a newspaper when I asked him to give it to a guard to pass on to me, and he did just that. I remember looking at a section that had slipped out as I tried to arrange it in my hands and on it I saw a drawing of the two spiralling strands of DNA. Under the drawing was a headline announcing that there had been a forensic science convention in Philadelphia which featured the newly discovered DNA fingerprinting technique being used, for the first time, to catch criminals in rape and murder cases.

As I sat down stiffly at my desk and continued to read, an amazing thought suddenly entered my head and I literally yelled out to my neighbour – the guy who had given me the newspaper – 'I'm holding the key to my cell in my hands!' He just laughed and said they must be giving out some really good pills these days to make me see things like that. Several of the others laughed, too. I laughed along with them, but only because I knew that this new DNA fingerprinting could do one thing: prove my innocence.

On Death Row you were entitled to make one phone call per month and you were allowed to speak for fifteen minutes as two guards with clubs stood over you as you talked into the phone piece held in your cuffed hands. The calls were very expensive and often not really worth the time, but it meant a lot to your family to hear your voice. With only two phones, bolted on to the wall beside the stairwell, shared between fifty Death Row men, you were lucky to get even that one call a month.

As soon as I had read that newspaper article to the point when I felt I knew every word off by heart, I put in a request for my monthly phone call so that I could call my attorney Joe Bullen and tell him that I wanted to use DNA testing to prove my innocence. As much as anything, I wanted to hear his reaction to me asking for a science to be used that could either prove me guilty or prove him wrong. I was sure he would either challenge me or patronise me and I was ready for it all. The block officers brought me out of my cell to use the phone on 26 February. It was a Friday and I was hoping that the letter I had sent to Mr Bullen the previous Monday informing him of my request to try and use DNA fingerprint testing had reached him. The phone connection was super slow but, as soon as I got through to him, I launched into telling him the initial steps I wanted him to take for me.

But he cut me short. He said he had received my letter the previous day and he had already spoken to the County Coroner, Dimitri Contostalavos.

Apparently, the Coroner was impressed by my willingness to try DNA testing, and, as all the sperm found during the autopsy of Mrs Craig was now in his care, he felt this was an excellent case on which to try out the new technique. Mr Bullen also told me that he had also spoken to the prosecutor now assigned to my case, and he too saw no reason to stop any testing, as he was clearly confident that this was a ploy on my part and he welcomed the chance to further prove my guilt.

I had psyched myself up for a fight with this man, believing that he would tell me not to waste his time, so now I felt suddenly deflated. I was unsure what to ask for next. But I gathered myself and asked him to speak to the lieutenant standing beside me and request that I be allowed to use the phone again to talk to him some more. I wanted to speak to him about this laboratory in New York State, which was using the new DNA testing procedure.

He agreed, saying that it was important we speak again on Monday, as he had to get written permission from the judge handling my appeals for this process to begin.

I handed the phone over to the lieutenant, who hung up having grunted a response to whatever it was Mr Bullen said to him. Then he turned to the guards who had brought me from my cell and told them to take me back. I tried to ask him to make sure a note was added to my files to say that I could make the call on Monday, but he just turned away and walked off as if I were an idiot for even asking him to respond to me. He was old school and, while he no longer ran the block as harshly as before, he had no time for the scum on Death Row. I did not push my luck by asking again and risk getting a smack in the mouth, so I went back to my cell just hoping that I would be allowed to make that phone call on Monday.

Meanwhile, I was looking forward to Jacque's visit on Sunday even more than usual. I really needed to talk to her. I had sent her the original newspaper article with the words 'We need to talk' scrawled across the margin. I wanted to tell her why it was so important that I tried DNA testing: not only was it my chance, it was fast becoming 'our chance'. Oh, how I wished for time to fly so that it was Sunday already and I could tell her why I had written those four words. I wanted finally to look her in the face and tell her that I had not killed another woman. I wanted finally to tell her that I had not raped that woman either. And science was going to prove this.

I exhausted myself with exercise and slept as much as I could in order to make time move forward as fast as possible. This wonderful new gift of hope had been handed to me out of nowhere and I had to use it.

But time passed that weekend just as slowly as it always does when you want the future to unfold quickly. As I waited impatiently for Sunday to arrive, I went through every imagined response to all I had to tell Jacque regarding the DNA testing article. For I knew this was either going to be the first step towards a new life together. Or I was about to take her for a ride through hell itself.

How do you look at someone and tell them that you did not murder or rape another human being, while inside you know that by telling them this you will only trap them in the battle to prove your innocence? I don't know what anyone else would have done, but I was filled with trepidation of the moment when I would have to tell Jacque the truth. And not just about the case, but about 'us' as well.

I had left so many things for Jacque to decide alone in the early part of our relationship. I hardly felt I was in the position to say much – I was at the mercy of both the prison administration and her willingness to drive so many hours to see me. And I had allowed us to grow close, despite my fears about the likely doomed outcome of our relationship.

But now, as I walked into that visiting room, I was being presented with the chance to tell the most important person in my life not only that I was innocent, but that I could prove it. For the first time since my return to Huntingdon, I had been sent a seemingly God-given new hope. And it had arrived just when, having reached as far as I could in my understanding of the world by myself, I had found a woman prepared to teach me how to develop as only a woman could. In this frightening yet empowering moment I felt there were so many symbols of fate and destiny pulling me towards a new future.

Sundays were very busy days, so it took a long time for visitors to get through the search process. However, they were allowed to bring in little things to pass the time with the inmate they were seeing. Jacque often brought a Scrabble set and we would just sit there and chat, the game providing a backdrop to our conversation as Jacque arranged my tiles according to my directions in their little holder facing the partition.

This Sunday there was nothing in her hands but a notepad and pen. She just walked in and said hello. Then, having touched fingers by pressing them through the metal screen between us, we sat down eagerly and both started to talk at once. Not only had she read the article I had sent to her, Jacque said, but she had been to the library and found some more articles and other materials, which she had copied for us to look at. It was obvious we needed a really good DNA expert, she rattled on, and we should also appeal to different organisations for help.

I couldn't stop smiling as she talked, while of course holding my cuffed hands up to my face in order to cover my missing teeth. She kept saying 'we' over and over – that's what made me smile. I managed to pause her long enough to say, 'I have two really big things to tell you. One is: I never even met Linda Mae Craig, so I had nothing to do with her rape or death. The second is: I know you are in love with me and I think I am in love with you as well.'

She wanted to make it easy for me, so she said, 'Why don't we worry about the *second* one, and leave the first one until later?' It was obviously the reverse thing to say, but that was the whole point. We both snickered as we shared our oh-so-clever way of allowing us not to linger on the fact that the words 'I love you' were out there finally.

Moving swiftly on, I told Jacque about how I'd shouted out loud when I'd read the article and Jacque said that when she'd mentioned it to Pam Tucker, Pam had told her there was a group in New York State called the Federal Defenders who were getting DNA cases tested and also that there were some new DNA labs there which specialised in rape cases.

I told Jacque all about my phone conversation with Joe Bullen and how he had surprised me with his positive response. She was so relieved to hear that my attorney was actually going to assist us in our efforts. There were tears and laughter and all sorts of things as we hatched our plans for the future.

For the first time, Jacque's leaving that day hurt me so much that I lay on my bed face down, crying bitterly. It hurt being that close to willing myself alive again. It hurt to think what I'd been through those past seven years before Jacque. It hurt just to think how I had nearly lost everything to hatred and anger. I was so grateful that I had met Jacque. This was surely the beginning of the end of my ordeal.

My fingers were cramped like you would not believe by that Monday afternoon when I got to make my phone call to Joe Bullen, as arranged. I had been writing letters all weekend to anyone and everyone in my life, telling them about this exciting new development with DNA testing and how I would have the chance to use science to overturn my conviction. My right hand ached as I flexed it over and over while holding the phone in my left, both hands cuffed in front of me. I must have looked like one of those crabs you see in nature shows, its oversized claws constantly on the move.

But I did not have a whole lot of time to dwell on what I looked like because as soon as I got through to Mr Bullen, he said simply, 'I got a phone call from the Delaware County Coroner who said they accidentally threw away all the autopsy material from this case.'

All I could do was stand there against the wall, still holding the phone to my ear, in chilled silence. Then I started trembling, before replying in a shaken voice, 'Please, Mr Bullen, don't do that to me.'

Mr Bullen responded angrily. He assumed – wrongly – that I was implying he had had something to do with the entire case evidence against me having been 'accidentally' thrown away. So we spent four or five minutes arguing over his part, or not, in my 'mental conspiracy' issues. He went on to tell me that the Coroner had managed to find two 'slide preparations' made from the autopsy evidence, which had not been thrown out; however, they were 'stained' with a solution that allowed them to be examined under a microscope but which would probably render them useless for our purposes. Nevertheless I should be grateful there were even these around, he told me, as if that were proof he had nothing to hide.

I started to shout that this was not about him, but about where the evidence was. The guards came and stood over me as I bellowed down the phone, 'This is so unfair! Only on Friday you said that the Coroner had the evidence and was on board with the testing and now you're telling me that in the span of three days it's all gone?' Then finally: 'How can I prove my innocence with those two "specks of nothing", as you put it, which have had chemicals poured all over them?'

As if talking to a particularly dim-witted child, Mr Bullen retorted that there was no reason for me to yell at him – as he had just done what I had requested and asked about 'these DNA things'.

I was beyond being mocked or condescended to by this man, so I continued shouting: 'Too bad you can't be proven wrong about my guilt by these DNA tests, as God forbid *you* could be wrong, you bastard!'

That was when one of the guards yanked the phone out of my hand. I had had my chance to act like a real live human being, one who could yell at others and have the luxury of getting angry – all this was pointed out to me forcibly as I had my hair yanked by the second guard as they both shoved me back towards my cell.

I boiled over with anger as they made sport of the words they had overheard me yell during my phone call. If they were capable of thought, I spluttered, they would realise what the obvious outcome to any DNA tests would be, and that was why the evidence had gone missing!

The guard who had yanked my hair – a tall, slender man – started taunting me by copying what I had been saying: 'Don't you see what DNA means?!' To which the other one – a very overweight man with a full facial beard typical of the men around Huntingdon – replied in this exaggerated 'Hillybilly' voice, 'Whoa! Slow down there, college boy! You need to just slow yer roll down, as yous can't jus' get up outta yer grave and go *home*!'

Now we were in front of my cell and they were both doing this 'retarded-person walk' routine with exaggeratedly stumbled and stuttered steps. By this time I was so angry that I could feel my stupid brain shutting down, as it always did. That, to me, was the worst humiliation of all. When people tormented me I just closed down, unable to defend myself. I lost all verbal skills and the ability to see out of my left eye as pain shot across my forehead. I had no clue what they were saying as they pushed me back into my cell. I was inside that part of my head, which used to eat me alive back then. I flung myself on my bed, defeated once more.

Only the previous day I had been lying on that bed aching for today to come. And now here I was covered in the tear stains of a whole new sorrow. I had no idea what to write to my parents or to Jacque or to any one of the other people I had just told about the DNA fingerprint testing. Lying there crying hot, angry tears was about all I had the energy for.

I knew my anger would get me back up on my feet, though, and that I would hurl that 'ball of fire' which was beginning to burn inside of my guts at someone. But right then I was as down as I could ever be and I had no will to do anything. I found myself sitting there on my bed until about 4 a.m. the next morning, reading voraciously through my trial transcripts, which were now scattered all about my feet. I was feverishly searching for any mention of semen or blood or of any other bodily fluid used as evidence during the trial. Somehow, I had to find out who else had been in contact with any of that evidence, as we needed every little bit we could find.

With there being only minuscule amounts of DNA left to analyse, I may not have the best tools to work with, I realised. I may not have money or the best law firms defending me. And the size of this challenge was so great that I could not possibly face it alone. The good thing was, though, that now I had Jacque fighting alongside me, saying how much she cared for me and loved me. I'll take those kinds of odds every time, I told myself.

Little did I know then, but my fight for DNA testing was to last fifteen long years. It was to become my ordeal within an ordeal. And I have never been so hurt nor so tested by any one thing as my fight to prove my innocence with science, and therefore to make others believe me.

Despite the early reality check on my efforts to have DNA testing, Joe Bullen did get the trial court to agree to send the contaminated slides off to a laboratory, in June 1988, to see whether they were suitable for testing. However, in August Cellmark diagnostics laboratories in Maryland confirmed that the two slides were indeed unusable.

On re-examining the trial transcripts, though, I found that some material from the autopsy had been sent to National Medical Associates (NMA) in Willow Grove, Pennsylvania, but had not been returned. Maybe I was in with a chance? I wrote to the lab's director, Vincent

Cordova, who responded personally to say that yes, they did indeed have some DNA evidence left over from my case. I had my misgivings about telling Mr Bullen of this development, but I did anyway, on the condition that he did not inform the prosecution until we had obtained the court's approval to use a new, improved DNA testing technique called Polymerase Chain Reaction, or PCR. But he ignored my request and told the prosecutor, Dennis McAndrews, who then sent two detectives, David Piefer and John Davidson, without a court order to NMA, allegedly in order to take these new DNA slides back to Cellmark.

The slides never arrived. Instead, they remained in the personal possession of Detective Davidson for the next two years as I tried – and failed – to get them handed over to the Coroner for testing/safekeeping.

Stung by this final betrayal by Mr Bullen, I filed a motion to have him removed from my case and the Delaware County court appointed Scott Galloway as my attorney instead. I was forced to represent myself in the hearing to have Joe Bullen removed in order to achieve this.

In June 1989 I again tried to file a motion by myself, this time for a new trial based on my own discovery that the police had found a pair of black leather men's gloves in Mrs Craig's car, the evidence for which had been improperly withheld before my murder trial. After hours of reading the trial transcripts, I had unearthed this fact in the so-called 'sidebar' transcripts – that is, conversations not heard by the jury, which took place between the trial judge and the defence and prosecution lawyers.

My motion went unheard in both the local court in Delaware County and the State Supreme Court of Pennsylvania. I had asked Mr Galloway to file it for me, but he refused, saying he did not want to alienate Judge William R. Toal Jr, who had assigned him to the case. Scott told me that Judge Toal had been a Delaware County prosecutor for twenty years before becoming a judge, and that his father had been a Delaware County prosecutor before him. When I asked Scott why it mattered so much who had assigned him to my case, he replied simply, 'The courthouse annexe is named for William R. Toal Sr. Do you *really* think you are going to get any kind of fairness from his son, the judge now handling your case, especially since his grandson, William R. Toal the Third, is a member of the prosecution team that is defending your DNA challenges?'

I appreciated his honesty, but felt that I was now completely left to my own efforts legally. It seemed that Scott Galloway was just a 'manager' appointed to a case no one else wanted to handle.

Eventually, I did file my own motion, based on my discovery about the gloves. I knew they were hugely important in tracing the identity of the real killer and I pursued this line of enquiry from my prison cell as best I could. But no files on the gloves existed, I was told, despite the fact that a police crime lab had examined and noted everything found in Mrs Craig's car. Insane. How could you collect all sorts of evidence, but have no files on that evidence? Also, what efforts had been made to determine whose gloves they were, given that the car had been found with its doors locked and the engine still running?

Having been turned down without a hearing by both the Pennsylvanian courts, my next step was to draw up a *habeas corpus* motion and seek help from the United States federal courts. This meant I was challenging my case at the highest level of appeal, the last one before they execute you. So, unlike other men on Death Row, who try to delay their approach to this last level of appeal, I was jumping ahead and seeking extraordinary relief to prove my innocence.

It took nearly two years of hard work on my part, but eventually the federal court ordered a hearing on the gloves and also on what the prosecutors knew about the missing DNA slides, which were, I pointed out, still in the personal possession of Detective Davidson. Dennis McAndrews, the Delaware County prosecutor, went before the Federal Court of Appeals in Philadelphia, saying that he had no knowledge of any gloves, and that no reference had been made to them prior to, during or after the trial. He denied that any files on the gloves existed and asserted that therefore no files had been withheld improperly.

He asked that my appeal be dismissed on the grounds that I was attempting to represent myself whilst being represented by a court-appointed attorney, Scott Galloway. It worked. The federal court accepted this and dismissed my appeal. However, the president judge of the court personally called defence attorney Peter Goldberger, of Ardmore, Pennsylvania, and asked him to take over my case as it related to the federal courts. A modest man and a former professor of law, he was the type of lawyer Death Row men dream of getting assigned to their case.

Meanwhile, back in Delaware County, Judge Toal ruled that it was up to the District Attorney to decide which laboratory to use for any future DNA testing. So, instead of having the best laboratory available to carry out the tests, as I had sought, it would be up to a newly opened police laboratory in Alabama, which had no previous experience of dealing with such materials.

I was returned to Huntingdon immediately after the Delaware County court ruling knowing that to try having any advanced form of DNA testing done would be a real joke. I was not being treated fairly, and I knew it. What lengths would these people go to to ensure I never had proper DNA testing done? Or never lived to tell this story?

14 'One riot at a time!'

There is an alternative version of reality I have witnessed that I cannot get out of my head. It is a secret world ruled by robotic creatures dressed in black, wearing plastic face shields and black metal helmets. And hidden within these costumes they do inhuman things I thought no normal human being could do . . .

As soon as I stepped off the van at Huntingdon following my last trip to court, I found I had other things to worry about besides DNA testing. Years of packing America's prisons with double the number of people that were supposed to be there meant they were about to explode. Pennsylvania's two dozen or so prisons were so overcrowded that violence was erupting on a daily basis. And that violence had reached boiling point. In October 1989, two of the state's prisons, Camp Hill and Huntingdon, were taken over by rioting inmates. This led to two back-to-back blood baths, both of which were to end in misery and death.

Over the usual noise of shouted conversations and banging radiators that I was used to hearing from my cell at night came the calls from other prisoners housed on the level above me. Through the outside windows facing their cells they could see there was some sort of disturbance going on in D-Block, a general population block housing over 400 men which faced B-Block. The Death Row men above me started yelling that they could see lights and movement and men fighting and running. Then smoke. Something big was happening.

Soon there were shouts from other men, reporting that they could see inmates fighting with staff. Someone heard screams for help from some guards out in the hallway. Next thing, we all started to smell the smoke coming in through the door at the rear of our block. Panic soon overtook the voices of the men yelling out above me as they saw fires being started, and more and more. Fire is the worst fear for men locked up in solitary. We all knew that in the middle of a riot no one was going to evacuate a hundred-plus Death Row prisoners. The staff would rather let us die than set free condemned men who might possibly join in the violence. The only people who would let us out were the rioters. But I dreaded that just as much, because as a so-called sex offender I could expect to be raped and beaten or even killed by these men.

I stood by my cell door picturing the faces of family and loved ones as they saw on their TVs that there was a prison uprising at Huntingdon. This was going to be big news, I thought aloud. Just then, the prison emergency siren, used to warn the local community, blared out overhead. If it blasted once there had been an escape; a continuous sound meant a state of emergency like a riot. But the locals didn't need a siren to tell them there was a riot going on. By now they could see the flames clearly over the prison walls as police and firefighters from all over were called in to help contain the spreading violence.

Meanwhile, back inside, the inmates had completely taken over D-Block. Having overpowered the guards, they had piled up some wooden furniture in one huge indoor bonfire and set fire to it in the hope of burning down the building's wooden roof, put there in the 1800s when the prison was first built. Less than an hour later the state governor ordered a rescue operation for the guards who had been overpowered by the rioting inmates.

State police, heavily armed and specially trained, were sent in to 'retake' D-Block, and they went about their task in a ruthless fashion.

As my cell was located on the ground floor I had some relief from the smoke that was seeping into B-Block in increasing levels. I covered my mouth with a water-soaked towel and sat on my cell floor just waiting for whatever might happen next. I had already wrapped all my best books and prized possessions in sheets and placed them on my bed, hoping to protect them. From my cell I could not see the fires, nor could I see the violence that was unfolding, but hearing the noise and smelling the smoke scared me no end. There are two long-standing jokes on Death Row: 'Never choke on your food while eating, as the guards are not going to come into your cell and do CPR on you', and: 'Never start a fire, as they will let you all burn to death before they try to rescue one killer locked up on Death Row'.

I don't know how long I sat there before I was drawn away from my cycle of thoughts by the distant sound of something being dragged along the cement floor at the other end of the block. In all my years of being locked up here on B-Block I had learned to recognise nearly every sound. It wasn't a mattress, as that made a kind of high-pitched hiss as the plastic coating scraped along the cement. But as it came closer, I realised I had indeed heard it before. Then I heard it again and again, coming closer and closer. And accompanying it was the rumbling crescendo of footsteps. No one was yelling out of their cells all of a sudden, I noticed. I stood up and looked out of my cell window as far as I could, just as some figures' back views came into sight. But these were not men wearing the grey uniforms of the prison guards; they were wearing black riot gear.

The first two figures were dragging the unconscious, bloody body of a prisoner. A white male, with several tattoos visible on his back and arms and wearing only a pair of brown prison-issue socks and white prison-issue boxer shorts, was being pulled along face down, his hands cuffed behind his back. His unconscious head was bouncing on the concrete floor like that of a deer I remember watching my father and brother drag through the woods on a hunting trip when I was a boy. In the next ten minutes, another twenty-five to thirty unconscious men were dragged by their ankles past my cell, a few completely naked. Some of them had blood pouring from open wounds on their heads and bodies; they looked horrifyingly dead as they bumped along the floor, their feet held together by giant plastic ties.

It was so eerie how all the macho yelling and calls for blood had suddenly died in the throats of my loud-mouthed companions on B-Block. It was so shocking to hear all those men on Death Row silenced by this gory procession. The bloody, urine-soaked trail it left was about four feet wide by the end of the night.

We all soon realised why the riot officers were dragging these men through B-Block. They had decided to lock them in the Death Row exercise cages. These first ones had been overpowered, knocked unconscious and then stripped before being dragged by their heels through our block. Next, as the entirety of D-Block became overwhelmed by thick, heavy smoke, all the remaining 400 or so men were just as efficiently collected up and dragged to the exercise cages.

I do not know what started the riot, other than the usual guard–prisoner conflict due to hundreds of men being locked up for too long in overcrowded conditions.

What I can tell you is that I rolled up my mattress on the floor by the door and sat astride it like a child sitting on a rolled-up taffy and watched, mesmerised, as one human being after another was dragged through the river of urine, blood and water that flowed outside my door.

It went on for hours. The sickening, wet-sliding sound of bodies being pulled along the floor which, combined with the harsh artificial light, the smell of smoke and the deep moaning of the siren, made it seem as if some crazy alternate reality had suddenly been flipped open or we were on the set of a horror movie. It was completely unreal. I sat there. I ate and I drank. I listened to music on my headphones. I cried and I laughed and I waited for another body to come by. What else do you do as near-naked human beings are dragged past your door for hours on end?

I was not being facetious previously when I described how I ate and drank throughout the night. It was not in celebration; I just wanted to stay awake and keep my strength up. I cried so much I made myself thirsty. But I wanted to be strong enough to handle whatever might happen next. As the cold daylight seeped in and made the images around me now seem all washed out, I too felt nothing.

I had met a madman with no soul in his eyes named James. I had seen the switch of insanity flip in Ted Bundy as he was lost to rage. But none of that had prepared me for this. I watched as these helmeted 'riot-bots' carried out their task in complete silence. They showed no anger, no hatred. They were just faceless creatures cleaning up after the mayhem of a riot with professional efficiency. And seeing how they could shut themselves off in order to do that also robbed me of my own ability to feel.

At the start of the incident, when I was not sure whether we would be burned alive or overwhelmed by rioting inmates, I had felt emotionally frayed and worn out. Now I had nothing left to feel; I had finally shut down.

Nonetheless I willed myself to stay there at my cell door, hoping to feel some emotion as I stood and watched the final scenes unfold. All I could think of was, what next? I knew for certain that I would be taken from my cell sometime in the next seventy-two hours and 'searched'. It was standard operating procedure following a major incident like this for guards to search the entire prison, cell by cell, for contraband. This was the only thing I could think of that made me feel anything. It worked. You can act like you are not afraid most of the time, but when you know there is violence coming your way and there's nothing you can do to stop it, you get scared.

I knew that I would be taken out of my cell by four guards who would then rip it apart. What they did to me while 'extracting' me would be determined by whoever was in charge of them; also, whether any staff had been killed or seriously hurt during the riot. I knew that, having checked my prison records and found I was a convicted rapist and murderer, they would be merciless. I had had guards act as if they actually saw me kill Mrs Craig themselves, the way they hurt me. I had seen what hatred combined with moral righteousness could do to them. My body still bears the scars, even if I have allowed my mind to let go of the pain I suffered for what they thought I was.

Before the guards arrived, I tried to memorise as much of my legal work as possible in case they tossed it all into the trash heap. I made lists in my head of which books I would beg them to let me keep.

I tried to work out my best strategy for what they would likely do to me. Run at them fast as they opened the door and hope it was over quick, or oil up the floor of my cell with soap and lotion, put up a long battle and wear them down? Either way, if I attacked them I would just end up being beaten up once again. So I decided to be passive, not put up a fight. I would take my chances and hope that the team of guards who came to search me was under proper supervision.

Guards having their eyes ripped out by inmates armed with deadly glass spears made out of four-foot-long fluorescent lights wrapped in bed sheets. Others being knocked unconscious and then sodomised with objects, or being stabbed by out-of-control prisoners. This is the violence we read about in the newspapers. What they call 'prison uprisings' or 'riots'. But then there is the violence that is only half talked about, that the public hardly realises goes on. This is the ugly truth for which that terrible word 'aftermath' is used, which is what goes on in marched procession as soon as the press have packed up their cameras and notepads.

In the 1990s Pennsylvania held criminal trials for the guards who had killed prisoners in the 'aftermath' of the Camp Hill and Huntingdon riots. A few of them went to prison themselves and a whole lot of prisoners had years added to their sentences for their parts in the uprisings. There were endless investigations and news articles written about the riots, their causes and effects. All the usual coverage.

But for me there was something missing from it all. I could never have imagined the guards' removed-from-it-all robotic manner that night if I hadn't witnessed it for myself.

My own response had also been to blank out emotionally. I wish that somehow we could have that riot played for us again on the big screen, translated into pixels and images, so that we could all judge our reactions to it better. Once, that is, the voice of some off-camera director had yelled, 'One riot at a time, please!' That way, maybe we would not be quite so numbed by the awful reality of what humans can do to each other.

It turned out that the day the 'search party' came to my cell, a young Hispanic guard named Ezekiel – known to everyone as 'Z' – was on duty. Z was not like so many of the other guards; he was somewhere between being regarded as an outsider by his co-workers and as an uneasy friend by the prisoners. I had grown to respect and like him, and he knew from handling my mail every day that I was fighting for DNA testing – sometimes he even asked me how I was getting on with my efforts to prove my innocence.

So when the other guards were just about to enter my cell, Z intercepted them. He muttered a few words and they stepped out of sight for a moment. As they did so, he turned to me and said in an urgent whisper, 'Nick, turn around and put your hands out through your pie hole so I can cuff you. Don't say anything and don't look at them as they search your cell. They won't do anything to hurt you if you say nothing.'

Tears welled in my eyes in gratitude for this kind gesture. I submissively turned my back, bent down and put my hands out through the five-inch-high, twenty-inch-long opening in my door so that Z could handcuff me. He then waited for my door to be opened remotely before guiding me by the arm out on to the walkway to wait by these huge bins full of inmates' property.

Mounds and mounds of debris – newspapers, magazines, shampoo bottles, deodorant roll-ons – lay strewn across the floor, having been tossed out in the search of the 145 cells on B-Block that day. Guards were filling up laundry carts with trash as the four officers went into my cell. I did not like to see my belongings ripped apart and I lost things that day that angered me, but, in truth, I was just glad I was spared from being beaten senseless. Many men endured far worse things than me that day. Thank God for a man like Z, who spared me one more day of pain.

15 Ten years gone

I met Jacque in December 1987. I married her on 1 July 1988 in a prison visiting room. The bridegroom wore handcuffs and two guards acted as witnesses. When it looked possible that DNA testing could prove my innocence and give us a realistic chance of being together, we decided to marry in the hope that we would be able to move on to happier times.

We honestly believed that DNA would set me free. For ten years Jacque drove the 225 miles from her world in Pittsburgh to mine in Huntingdon, six days a month, as we engaged in protracted legal battles to have the testing carried out.

Jacque left me in 1997, unable to take any more denials by the courts. Five inconclusive DNA tests meant there was not going to be a happily ever after. She divorced me finally in 1998, having found someone new in her life. In the ten years of our relationship, we experienced one hell of a ride through every emotion a couple could feel, locked as we were in our huge legal battle.

In 1988 the only known uncontaminated DNA evidence had been taken by Detective Davidson; it was later destroyed.

In December 1989 my direct appeal against the death sentence was denied and all claims that my original trial had been unfairly held were dismissed by the State Supreme Court of Pennsylvania.

In June 1990 the victim's clothing, worn at the time of her murder, was finally located by a former evidence custodian in the Delaware County courthouse evidence room.

In June 1991, a year after Mrs Craig's clothing had been found, we finally persuaded a lab to extract samples of sperm taken from her underwear.

In November 1992 all my appeals in the federal courts were dismissed and I was forced to accept DNA testing of the samples by an inexperienced newly opened police laboratory in Alabama.

In July 1993 the first DNA testing by the Alabama laboratory came back 'inconclusive' due to degraded evidence.

In September 1993 I discovered that not all the evidence had been sent to the Alabama lab and there were six tubes of extracted sperm-based DNA still held by Cellmark laboratories. I finally got the Federal Defenders Office to support my DNA efforts, including having Michael Wiseman and Christina Swarns to take over the DNA costs from the federal courts.

In January 1995 Huntingdon's Death Row was finally shut down and I was sent to Pittsburgh.

In June 1995 I was allowed representation by the Federal Defenders Association through the help of Peter Goldberger and was given access to their capital defence funding in order to appeal in the federal courts.

In 1996 I sought to have the unshipped evidence at Cellmark labs finally sent to a properly qualified DNA laboratory.

In August 1997 I won the right in the federal courts to have all of the tubes of evidence at Cellmark sent to the highest qualified lab in the USA, Forensic Science Associates in California, for PCR-enhanced DNA testing.

In September 1997 the killer's gloves were finally released by the prosecutor and sent to Cellmark for shipment to FSA, along with six tubes of DNA.

In November 1997 the package sent to FSA by Cellmark broke open, rendering the evidence useless.

Despite this long battle, between the years 1988 and 1998 I was as happy as anyone on earth, because I was totally convinced I was not alone. I was no longer meandering through life by myself and I believed that the power of love would help me find all my best qualities. Not only that, but I would try to live by everything I now held most dear. For ten years I was able to feel no hurt if this person or that person attacked me for why I was in prison. I had a whole other world, which I had made with another person, Jacque. In every letter, every phone call, we shared my ordeal, and that gave me a sense of protection that I had never felt before.

I was so grateful to Jacque for witnessing how my battle for DNA testing had become such a test of will power. I might have stayed happy if it were not for the fact that as time went on I realised that our fight was eating into her and was in danger of tearing down our love. This wonderful person, who was my lodestone on every step of my way through the legal maze, had become trapped in my world – and it was me who was holding her there. But time ignored both of us. I blinked and ten years, thousands of miles driven, hundreds of letters written and greeting cards with photographs tucked inside them sent, were suddenly yesterdays for me. I watched horrified as the stupid desperate mess I had made of my life as a young man came back to cause her so much pain. That is still the most terrible thing I have ever done in my life: I let someone keep coming to see me for years and years when I now see that I was using her to carry me.

I remember vividly that day in December 1997 when Jacque walked into the prison visiting room for the last time. By then I had been transferred to the Western State Penitentiary at Pittsburgh, as a commission had recognised what a hellhole Huntingdon's B-Block was and had had it shut down. We just sat there the first few moments, but I knew what was coming. The previous month, my nine-year attempt to have tested both the killer's gloves and all remaining DNA recovered from the sperm found on the victim's underwear had failed when it had been damaged in shipping. Cellmark had screwed up badly and seemingly lost all known evidence. They had not prepared the package properly and it had split open on its way to a lab in California. Six centrifuge tubes full of evidence were deemed contaminated. Edward Blake, the director at Forensic Science Associates in California, who were due to test it, would not test the spilled evidence, so any realistic chance I had of having DNA testing was over.

That day, none of this mattered. Jacque had warned me on the phone that there was something she wanted to tell me and I knew what that something was going to be. And now here at Western State she just laid it all out, saying, 'Nicky, I cannot *do* this any more! It is stealing the life out of me. I have a house full of legal boxes on this case. My mom is now gone and I am so alone. I have met someone else and I think I want to be with him. He don't want me to see you any more, so I can't come back after today.'

It was so lame that we were having such an important and intimate conversation in the communal visiting booth used by both Death Row and high-security prisoners. It was just a twenty-foot-long aquarium-like glass enclosure with, on the prisoners' side, four stools bolted to the floor. And right next to me was another inmate, cooing to his 'boo', as he kept calling his overweight, scantily clad female visitor.

It so crushed me that my last moments with the person to whom I had clung so hard were to be shared with such a cheap example of humanity. I was holding on to the thick black phone receiver on my side of the glass so fiercely that Jacque could see I was likely to do something drastic and implored me with her eyes not to. When you spoke into the phone it magnified your voice in this cheap, tinny way as it transmitted your every word over a small network to a guard sitting in a booth fitted with one-way glass, just twenty feet away. It was so degrading to know that there was this faceless witness to the dying moments of our love. It took every bit of my willpower to do nothing. To just sit still and hold back the tears was a huge effort. I was so grateful I was holding the phone at the far end of the visiting room, so I could hunch down to my right and talk without too many other people seeing my face.

Jacque and I laughed awkwardly and for a moment we were both filled by the warmth of our old roles in which we shined brightly as a united couple. But then I broke down, I let it out, I sobbed, and the asshole next to me, who had been rubbing himself under the counter while his girlfriend talked to him, stopped long enough to look at me. I blazed him to incinerated dust with the expression on my face. He ducked sideways and whispered a few things to his girlfriend before moving to a phone further away from me that barely worked at all. He kept whispering and casting nervous glances at me to see if I was going to cash his chips in for him early. I needed someone to take out my hurt out on and, handcuffed or not, I would have beaten him until all my strength had gone if he had said a single word to me. Luckily for him, he did not.

Now I looked again at Jacque and how time had taken such a chunk of her youth. If only I had had the courage to look in the glass I would also have caught a glimpse of my own time-stolen image.

But I was proud, too, of what we had achieved together. Back in 1988, I had become the first man on Death Row in the USA to ask for DNA testing. In the beginning we had no idea what it was we were asking for, but we had learned so much. And for ten tireless years Jacque had been my partner in our battle to be heard, wearing my death sentence like a badge of honour.

Finally when I could talk I began: 'I have all the resources that federal court funding has allowed me, I have five lawyers lodging appeals on my behalf because the evidence was spilled, and *now* you wanna quit?'

We both cracked smiles as we slipped into the trademark joking style of our relationship. I continued the jocular mood with: 'Yo, you remember back in 1993 when we were forced to use the Alabama Police Department of Forensic Services for our first DNA tests and they used up what we thought was all the evidence on their "inconclusive" results?'

Jacque got into the spirit of our performance by adding in this pseudo-female TV reporter voice: 'Let's not forget how it took six long years to get the District Attorney to hand over the killer's gloves that were, oh by the way, hidden from your lawyers during your trial!'

I added to the hamming-up with an imitation of an old 1970s TV show, *Rowan Martin's Laugh-in:* 'And now, a word from our sponsors, "Grind 'Em Up and Kill 'Em All

Prosecutors", proud makers of elected officials all over the United States of America . . .'

Those were our last few moments of real laughter before I jumped into talking about the real business of why she was here. I tried to be upbeat and positive. I told her that I was glad for her that she had met someone else, even as it made me cringe inside.

I told her how grateful I was that she had been prepared to come and hear me bitch and whine about my crappy life – which drew a small laugh as she tried to hide her now-flooded eyes. I said everything I was supposed to say. And I did everything I could to reassure myself that it was all true. That I could go on without her. I may have had feelings of bitterness that she was leaving, but I tried so hard to spare us both this hurtful truth.

Even though I realised it was our constant fight that had brought us closer together, I saw too that it was this final spillage which had just stolen Jacque's will to go on. It sickened me that, in the end, it was my own rotten luck that had cheated us out of a new life. I could not visualise the lab assistant who had packed the box improperly; I could not conjure up hate for the innocuous delivery person who had knocked the package about. All I could see right now was the face of someone who had had enough of this endless nightmare and who knew that only more madness followed if she stayed.

We sat in that visiting booth for a little while not really saying a whole lot. I tried discreetly to look at Jacque's watch as she held the phone up to her ear. Over an hour had passed already. And yet I could not imagine another hour in my life that would be filled with so much human emotion or go so slowly.

I could tell from her face I hurt her by asking if she loved this new man. And I hurt her some more by asking if she thought he loved her as much, or if they were going to get married. She said she really did not know. But we both knew she was lying to try and spare us both. As we bounced away from this line of questioning, I broke down and pleaded with her to 'just go now, please'.

I turned to look away and she got up and moved off towards the door. I stood up and banged the hell out of my knees on the lip of the counter, but at least I was filled with the warmth of pain as I saw her pick her way speedily through the chairs filled with visitors. I knew it was pointless to shout, as I was behind two inches of security glass, so I just let the phone slip on to the countertop and clang there on the metal. When I could no longer see her, I pressed my face into the cold concrete wall and wept like a child who had lost its comfort blanket.

I don't even remember how I got back to my cell that December day. I just recall staring out of my window, up on the fifth floor, and watching the snowfall under a streetlight as I sat there transfixed by the thoughts that played out in my head. Had she ever really existed? Had I really been in love or had I just been using her? How would I ever face everything without someone else there to carry my burden?

I sat listening to WYEP, a Pittsburgh radio station, endlessly on my headphones. It was all I could do just to listen to music and hope to hear a song that would help me recall the good things Jacque and I had once shared. I heard the song I wished for, 'Ten Years Gone' by Led Zeppelin. I cry even when I hear it now.

No words can explain what Jacque's leaving did to me. I had to face the fact that I had once been so close to a chance at life, but it had been snatched from me. And I had to carry on by myself, without the one person who had said that, no matter what, she would never leave me to die here alone. She had sworn she would sit by me to the end and watch me be executed. She lied. I had sworn I would always love her. I lied, too.

16 All the pictures on the wall

Soon after Jacque left me I received a card from a 'lay chaplain' who worked in a hospital. She explained in a note folded neatly into the card that her name was Maria (this isn't her real name, as she has asked to be kept anonymous) and she was a grandmother who had recently read Sister Helen Prejean's book titled *Dead Man Walking*, about her encounters with men on Death Row. Now, she said, she wanted to get involved in Death Row issues because this book had made her realise how wrong the death sentence was.

When I received that card I responded by saying that I was glad for the offer but I was not interested in being her pen pal. She then wrote to me a second time saying her hospital was quite near to the prison and that she would come by and see me if I did not write back. The way she put it, she was going to come to the prison anyway and sort out why I did not understand her. To her it was so plain: she had read this book and now she wanted to get involved in capital punishment issues, whether I liked it or not. She added that she and her friend Sister Grace had decided that, as my name was near the end of the alphabet, I was a good person to start with as I probably was overlooked.

I was in no mood to bear the brunt of some do-gooder's efforts to hold hands with the guilty right before they are executed. I had just lost all reason to believe I had any chance of using DNA testing to prove my innocence, and the one person whose help I had relied on more than anyone else's had just left me. I tossed the letter into the corner of my cell along with the piles of everything else that lay scattered on the floor and laughed at this foolish woman. Who the hell was she to think I was so desperate to see someone from the outside world that I would just open up to her merely because she had been enlightened by some book?

I had been hiding in my bed for days following that ugly day when Jacque had said farewell. I was using sleep as a way of hiding from the horrible reality that I could be stuck here in prison for the rest of my life. My attitude was sour and I was not talking to anyone. I had even let my guard down against those around me who could harm me. One person in particular that I ran foul of was a guard named Daniel Daily, aka 'Double D'. There are some men who should never be allowed to become prison guards. Among them are former police officers who have been fired from the force for alcoholism or other abuses. He was one of those. As a former police officer, he had arrested men who then became prisoners, and he perceived us as predators on society and dealt with us accordingly. He was a man who brought hatred in to work with him every day like it was his lunch pail.

He was always calling me his 'favourite rapist-murderer' whom he held in such 'esteem' compared to all the others that he 'had love for', as he put it. When he fed me or gave me my mail or did any of the endless little things that have to be done for a man in solitary confinement, he constantly reminded me that I was a toy for his amusement.

On one particular day I was feeling so bitter about Jacque that I 'barked' at him, as they say. When he commanded me to move my boxes of legal work out on to the walkway, I snapped back at him as I reached down for them at my own good pace.

For my nasty few words, he slammed the cell door on to my left hand, which I had been too slow to get out of the way. He broke seven bones. Weirdly, though, I was quite happy to feel physical pain so bad that it stole away all the emotional agony I was feeling. I used to beat my head against the wall of my cell for much the same reason. So, for all the anger I felt towards that man for his cruel and cowardly act, I was glad for what he had done.

I joined right in on my own misery as I really did not care. I went into a rage. I tore my belongings to shreds, daring him to go get the extraction team. Seeing as how it was him who had caused me the physical damage that would generate the paperwork that could lead to an investigation, 'Double D' walked quietly off the unit, closing the outer door behind him so that none of the administration team could hear my ranting.

As soon as I lost the rest of my anger and strength, I sat down and filled in a grievance form in which I formally charged 'Double D' with assault. I knew what I was doing: there would be an investigation and from then on I was doomed. No one wants to be the 'rat' who tells on the very people who are feeding you and caring for you even as they lock you in your cell. But I couldn't care less. I asked to be transferred to Greene County prison, supposedly the new 'scariest place' for Pennsylvania to lock up its miscreants. I knew that at the time I was asking to go there, its entire Death Row population was on a hunger strike in protest at abuse by guards.

So what? I would make sure that this man 'Double D' understood there was one person who was prepared to stand up to him. When he saw a copy of my grievance form, he was not happy. But I was not foolish. I also sent copies to my lawyer and to the Commissioner of Corrections.

I was brought before an investigative panel, which decided to grant me my wish and ship me to Greene County prison. I would be sent there right after the coming new year of 1998, they decided, as soon as a Death Row prisoner from that prison was found who could be transferred to Pittsburgh in exchange for me. I had won my small battle against this tyrant, but still I sat in my cell sulking, with nothing to provoke me out of my bleakness. I just went slowly back into self-induced hibernation, sleeping and 'zoning out' in front of the television. I even craved drugs for the first time in so long – although, in that respect, I was glad I was on Death Row, as that actually protected me from what I would have surely done to myself with drugs or booze had I been in the prison's general population.

At about the same time I received that Christmas card from 'Maria', I received another one, from my mother. It was very cute and sweet, but even she could not manage her usual, falsely upbeat message along the lines of 'Next year we will all be together for the holidays.' It was clearly too hard for her to fake it following the devastating news of the contamination of the DNA evidence. So, instead she wrote that she was relieved that Jacque was right there in Pittsburgh to support me. Ouch.

Telling my mother that my marriage was over was going to have to wait until later, I told myself. Maybe in the spring, it would be best to tell them.

In jail, you sort of try to 'time it' when to share bad news. Not during the holidays. You don't want to ruin those special times for people on the outside. Families mark each holiday as a reinforcement of hope and pray for your return. Meanwhile, inside prison, you just pray it will pass as quickly as possible so that you can tell your family some new terrible piece of news they will have to cope with.

Peering over the top of my mother's card as I sat reading it in bed, I saw again the card from the hospital worker and picked it up off the floor. Then I went over to my coffee-stained desk, moved my papers out of the way and got out pen and paper in order to write a short note to this Maria woman. I began:

Hello Maria,

My wife of ten years recently left me and since she was the only person who bothered to come and see me regularly, my social calendar just got a huge opening.

I hope you do come by soon so that we can find something interesting to talk about, like the dying patients you watch over, or we can have a lovely chat about Death Row prisoners who play-act the last moments of killing their victims to entertain us all whenever the power goes out . . .

I knew that most of what I wrote to Maria was self-directed taunts that hurt me even to see them written on paper. I was also hoping to scare her off with my facetious-ness. I preferred to address such a hurtful letter to a stranger than write a truthful one to my mother.

I regarded it as the lesser of two hurts. I was not unaware, though, that this innocuous person did not deserve my anger or sarcasm. Nonetheless there was a smirk on my face as I dropped the letter into the slot in my door so that it could be picked up by the guard. I noted with a bit of an upturned chin how mailing that letter made me feel better. Like a crab in a bucket full of other crabs, I reached out and pinched anything in sight.

It was two days before Christmas and I had no expecta-tion of ever hearing back from Maria when I got an unexpected visit from the Catholic priest who worked in the prison. I had never even spoken to him before, as I was not a Catholic; in fact, I had had no contact with representatives of any of the organised religions within Pittsburgh prison. However, I recognised him from when he had come on to the unit previously to perform services for those who requested them.

Today he stopped by my door just long enough to say, 'I received a phone call from your spiritual adviser.' Then he held up a piece of paper and read out: 'Mrs Maria. She said she'll be here to see you at 2 p.m. tomorrow, "if you have time". Also, she asked me to ask you if you want me to perform a service for you.'

'Yes, I have time,' I replied. 'And no, I don't need anything from you, thank you.'

Then, before leaving my door, the priest said: 'Do you acknowledge Maria as your spiritual adviser and should I note her down as such?'

I told the priest, 'Yes, please go on and do just *that* for me.'

He seemed a bit unsure how to take this comment, but he let it go.

I did not bother to tell him that I had never met this woman before in my life and that, as far as I knew, she could be some crazy person who was just saying she was a 'lay chaplain', or whatever it was she did.

I kind of liked the idea that the whole thing was already a running joke. And I would find out shortly what an actual visit from this person would be like. According to the rules, as my adviser she was officially allowed to attend my execution! I thought it sort of cute how she had already achieved the role she wanted, just like her new favourite author, Sister Helen. All that was needed now was some overblown orchestral music playing in the background as they strapped me to a gurney ready for execution – and her imagined scenario would be complete.

When I was brought into the visiting room the next afternoon, I saw a woman sitting alone opposite an unoccupied prisoner's stool. I was once again in the aquarium-like booth, but today there were no other prisoners occupying it. As I passed through the small metal door on the prisoner's side of the booth I immediately felt as if I were on display, with twenty sets of eyes looking at me. I walked over in front of the woman and picked up the phone. She looked up at me curiously as I encouraged her to do the same. She was a middle-aged woman wearing a white blouse under a brown suit. Her shoulder-length hair was reddish brown and she wore no make-up. She looked professional. As soon as she lifted the phone to her ear, I said, 'So, you got any "adviser-like" things to say to me?'

The woman looked me right in the face and said, 'I am here to see Richard So-and-so. You are not him.' To which she added the obvious, 'I think you may have thought I was someone else.'

I checked her eyes to see if this was a put-on, as for a second there I thought this might be Maria responding to my stupid joke. It soon dawned on me, though, that I really had walked up to a complete stranger and come out with this tired-ass line. Now I had to move. I gathered up the scattered remains of my dignity and slid over two stools to the stool furthest away from her.

As I covered my left eye in shame, half turning from view, I cringed and shrivelled up inside. I looked through my laced fingers to see how many possible witnesses there had been to my brilliant moment.

Now I noticed a woman seated to my right who looked up from the book she was reading. She got up and came over to the chair in front of me. She looked to be in her mid-fifties, with long hair. She smiled at me as she picked up the phone on her side of the glass and began to speak. I figured that this time I'd better wait and see who I was talking to before I made another stupid blunder. The woman introduced herself as Maria and apologised for not already being in the visitors' booth before I arrived. She said that she had found this fascinating book over on a shelf. All the visitors' rules were laid out in it, including the one that any prisoner 'caught having sex' with a visitor would lose all visiting privileges. I nodded, like it was obvious that people have sex in the visiting room and don't care who's there with them or what the penalty is. She seemed to think it was weird that they actually had to write down a rule expressly forbidding it.

Then she explained that she had become so caught up in reading the rule book that she had simply sat down in the chair she was standing next to without thinking. I was so relieved she had not seen what I had just done to

Richard So-and-so's visitor that I missed her eager attempt to get me to smile.

Before she could go any further, I interrupted her by saying how the prison chaplain had come by to tell me that he was putting her name down as my spiritual adviser, so I hoped she was at least as well qualified as a 'spiritual adviser' as she was in her hospital job – if she really *had* that job.

She calmly asked me what I meant by that last bit, but I replied that I had been caught off-guard by the priest asking me about my spiritual adviser, especially as I'd never met her. I said I found this whole notion of appointing someone as your spiritual coach in order to help you become closer to God before meeting your death was all very simple-minded. Wouldn't it be funny if she turned out to be a nutcase who just pretended to work in a hospital!

At that Maria just laughed and, despite myself, I liked her right away. She was obviously a genuine person who had been struck hard by what she had learned from that book about the treatment of prisoners on Death Row. It had never really occurred to her that she couldn't do what she had set out to do: find someone on Death Row, go to see them, then appeal to them to find the best in themselves before leaving this world.

I liked how every effort I made to be difficult, indeed my conforming to her over-simplified view of what Death Row prisoners were like, only made her smile even more. At one point, I said, 'How the hell can you work all day in a hospital surrounded by dying people and *not* be emotionally drained by all that pain and suffering?'

At which she looked me right in the eye and said, 'How the hell can you live with the ones who put some of those people who are dying in my care and not be filled with anger over what they did?'

Good point. I was going to leave the matter at that, but then Maria seemed to withdraw into herself. I waited until whatever thoughts she was wrangling with let her alone before asking, 'You OK over there, or do you need a moment?'

A lot of thought was obviously going into what she was winding herself up to say next – either 'Goodbye' or something really serious. I could see she was someone who went softly through life, making few demands on others. So now I wiped any hint of a smile off my face and waited for her to compose herself.

Eventually Maria folded her hands on her lap and looked at me as if searching for the best approach. Then she continued quietly, 'I have only one thing, really . . . they bring to our hospital inmates from this prison that have been stabbed or hurt. You *have* to promise me that you will not hurt anyone while we are friends, as I cannot bear to think of someone coming into my hospital unit that you have hurt.'

As she spoke she had been looking at the bandages on my hand from where 'Double D' had broken it. I had no clue what she already knew about me from either the priest or whoever else she had talked to, but I was not there to tell her my business. In truth, I was stung a bit by her words, as I had not expected someone to come here and confront me, however gently, about my bitterness. I had barely talked to anyone in the past month, so I was not about to start making promises to this woman I'd only just met.

I said simply, 'I wish you *were* my "friend", as you put it, as friends are few and far between for me these days.' We both smiled and she let the comment pass. She was like a parent waiting patiently for a child to come up with the answer to a difficult question. I didn't duck her question, though; I simply waited a few moments before saying, 'I don't know what I am capable of at this point, honey. Maybe you should wait and see if you really want to be my friend first.'

Was this a serious battle of wills or just a temporary blip in the progress of a possible friendship? She did not seem too put off by my reply as she sat there in silence. Then I realised that she was trying to force me to make a choice – and I was not in the mood to be polite.

'*What?!*' I shouted into the phone, looking at her hard through the glass. I also made an up-and-down motion with my shoulders, demanding she say now whatever she wanted to say. She did nothing. She just sat there looking up at me – I had stood up by now – her eyes locked on mine. I was getting really annoyed, but I repeated in a softer voice: 'What?'

She started again. 'I just feel it would be such a waste of time if I came here to help you and then you hurt someone else.'

At this I put the phone down on the counter. I wanted to say to her: 'How dare you come here and hurt me like this, lady?' or 'Who do you think you are with all your quiet self-assuredness and telling me what the hell I should do?' I was so filled by a thousand brutal things I wanted to say to hurt her. But my cheeks were also burning with the salt from my tears as I let them roll down my face. All I could see was this blurred image of a woman as I thought about how hard I had tried to be what she wanted me to be long before I met her. And here she was wanting to turn me into something I had already become well before she ever read her damn book. All I had to say to her was 'Goodbye'.

Then, as all those words came blurting to my lips, I saw it. I saw that I really *had* become those things. I had felt the love of another and I had used it to grow up as a man. I had lived and loved openly as I had tried to let go of my anger, even as I was being cheated out of hope. I started to cry again, this time with tears of recognition. I really had tried to be good for my mom and dad. I had tried for Jacque. I had tried for the men whom I had helped get through this hell and who had become my friends. I already had every reason to hold my head up again as a man. I had nothing to prove to myself and, I realised, you can never really prove yourself to the world. Yes, as far as she was concerned, I was a man who had raped and killed and she was here to find what good there was left inside him. But I had already found it – though it had taken my encounter with her for me to realise that I had done so.

I wiped the tears away and smiled back at her. Then I said, 'I swear to you that if you come back to see me and become my friend, no matter what I have to do, I will never hurt another human being while I am in here.'

Now it was her turn to cry. She said she wanted to go to the ladies' room, but now that we had both gotten over 'this tough part' we could 'start over' once she came back.

Yet again, she was so straightforward in what she said and how she said it. No clutter of thoughts conflicted her – 'just say it and then do it' was her attitude. And suddenly I felt OK with this. I just needed to get myself back together before she came back from the ladies' room.

When Maria returned, we awkwardly started to talk again on the phones. Since she first wrote to me, she said, she had looked out for topics we might discuss. Then she brought out of her pocket a plastic coin purse in which she had placed a neatly folded piece of paper. On the paper was a list. She skimmed through it and began: 'Do you believe in God?'

'Yes,' I replied.

She seemed unsure whether to challenge me on this, so she hesitated briefly before asking me the next question. 'Do you have a hobby?'

I told her I had just begun teaching myself the art of making transfers on to handkerchiefs.

'Oh good,' she said. 'Sister Grace will like that.'

I began to wonder what hold the mysterious Sister Grace had over this woman. She then agreed that, in exchange for her getting me art supplies, I would give her one of my handkerchiefs. She also said that she would be happy to share books with me, but I told her that I was giving reading a break these days, as I wanted my eyes to take it easy for a while.

Next question. 'When I come here again, do you want me to think of funny stories to share with you, or should we stick to serious subjects?'

Funny stories appealed to me. 'I can tell you all sorts of funny things that happen in this place, so let's make it a two-way traffic and keep us in a light mood!'

Straight-faced, she sat there for a second before responding, 'Oh good, then you and I can just talk normally about everyday life when I come back to visit.' Then, as we realised how far from everyday both our lives were, we burst out laughing.

She wrote down 'Funny stories (ha, ha)' on her bit of paper and I smiled as she did so, imagining her recalling amusing things to tell me when she came back. For, yes, I hoped that she would come back. I wanted to tell someone outside that life in prison was not always so horrible. I needed someone whose own job was so ugly that they could laugh with me and not at me. I just hoped that this person would show me some care now when I really needed it. For just that alone, I'd have danced around like a circus creature.

I went back to my cell and looked at the photos of family and friends I had stuck up on the wall. I knew which year I had taped which one where. I knew the exact time sequence of all the family gatherings I had not been able to attend. I noticed the gap when someone was missing from a photo. I had memorised every image from having sat and looked at them thousands of times and I just knew in my heart that each was a small lie. None of these photographic images was a close likeness of how that person looked right now. Even the previous six months would have changed them.

It was time now not to live for all those pictures on my wall. Instead, I would start living for the here and now, through which maybe I would find peace of mind. I had no more fight left inside me to chase the DNA testing.

I'd even allowed my lawyers to file mental health claims for my death sentence to be overturned on the grounds of diminished responsibility. Before that, I'd never once asked for life imprisonment instead of a death sentence; yet I'd done it all for the sake of getting the money for the DNA tests which hadn't been allowed anyway after the tubes were damaged in transit. I had been through the humiliation of being made to surrender my principles and ask for mercy for something I had not done in order to get testing that had not happened.

Now I wanted to find out what was inside of me that was not tied to others. I wanted to discover what was waiting for me in death. It amused me that I was going on such a huge journey with such a shaky-looking navigator as my 'spiritual adviser', but I was even worse off in my own company, alone in my cell.

17 'We ain't got no Spanish books on spying!'

After three years in Pittsburgh Penitentiary I was ready for a change. At first I had really enjoyed having a window in my cell. I recalled fondly how, when I was first moved there in January 1995, I would sit for hours just looking out on to the real world through my brand-new window. I thought that at Pittsburgh I would be able to move on from all the dark memories of my twelve brutal years at Huntingdon . . .

But in many ways Pittsburgh was no better. Death Row was located in a sealed unit for which the only source of air was an artificial ventilation system. In summer you froze and in winter you baked. Air – sometimes cold, sometimes hot – pumped out of the wall all day every day. After a while of living like this you could detect the tiniest new smell that floated your way. Also, your ears became deadened to the constant white noise of the air coming out of the vents 24/7. Your eyes also became so used to the fluorescent lighting of your cell that you could not handle natural sunlight when you were taken outside for exercise.

Human skin cells make up eighty per cent of indoor dust. In many prisons they do not change the hepa-filtration filters in the air vents, as they are too expensive to replace, so you end up with this micro-fine dust being constantly blown about your cell. When you get up for the 'head count' in the morning you can see your footprints in the dust that has settled on the floor overnight.

In a new Death Row unit like the one in Pittsburgh, built in the 1990s, which is sealed shut and filled with dry, vented air, you end up being preserved like a mummy. Your skin becomes taut. Your sinuses are always full of powdery grit, as are your eyes. I even began to miss the times when I could smell the rain back in Huntingdon. For, whenever the rear door to B-Block was opened and fresh air poured in from outside, the wind would sweep in all these smells of nature. I missed that, I really did. I did not like how in Pittsburgh nothing seemed to change. It felt like I was in one of those controlled experiments in which everything has to be the same all the time.

Maria started coming to see me once a week, on her way either to or from work. All through January and February 1998, as I nervously waited out the time it took for my transfer to Greene County prison to come through, she visited me. I really was so grateful to have this wise and serene woman calmly walk into the wreckage of my life and just *listen*. By now, also, I knew that I had nothing to prove to her. And she quickly applied her professional skills as a grief counsellor to help me accept my very difficult situation, and made me start thinking seriously about the possibility that my life could end there.

The best thing about having someone to talk to whose job it is to counsel the families of the dying is that you know they are a deeply genuine person. I could never imagine doing Maria's job. I found it amazing that she worked with the same heartbreak every day and yet she did not walk around in tears.

Through listening to Maria, though, I grew to have so much respect for anyone who works in a hospital. You know that death is a likely outcome for the patients you care for and sometimes the only reason they are alive at all is because they are hooked up to some machinery. You look into the crying faces of family members as someone they love slips away from them. You share in their grief. Then you go home and talk to your grandchildren on the phone or you laugh with your daughter who thinks you are God's gift to her children who adore you. And you are. You really are.

Maria was such an easy target for my humour, and I quickly fell for hers. Neither one of us wanted just to sit there and trade tales of gore and suffering. We both wanted to share our ability to look at life *differently*, as a way also of rising above our day-to-day surroundings. I was delighted to have found someone with whom I could laugh so openly. I had such a wonderful time thinking of quips to make to her while she was in the middle of a serious discussion about the Catholic spiritual writer Thomas Merton or the Buddhist freedom rights leader Thich Nhat Hanh. But I also knew that, at the heart of it all, she was trying to find out if there was still inside of me the will to remain what I thought I had become.

Oddly enough, those 'funny stories' did often come up naturally in the middle of serious discussions. Prison was such a foreign world for Maria that she was fascinated by every little detail of life on Death Row. Things I would not think to mention. For instance, how do you punish someone on Death Row?

I told her that if a man on Death Row was placed on 'disciplinary time', he had his privileges taken away. These might be the TV he had purchased through the prison commissary store, or all his artwork and personal items, until he was left with the bare minimum: two towels, two sheets, one blanket, one pillowcase, one cut-handled toothbrush (no more than two inches long), one tube of toothpaste, one comb, one bible or other religious book, one pair of shower slides, one pair of eyeglasses. He would then be issued with three sets of underclothes and a bright orange jumpsuit with special markings on it to identify him as a disciplinary-timed inmate.

Maria wanted to know about reading material. I told her that while on disciplinary time you were at the mercy of the 'Death Row library'; that is, a bunch of cast-offs from the prison's main library which were sent over from time to time. The worst part of it was that, because they left it up to the guards to distribute the two books per week you were allowed, it went 'wrong' sometimes.

I was smiling when I said this, so she wanted to know what I meant. I drew myself up and let go. I knew that Maria was the one person who would find it funny when I told her. And, damn it, I missed laughing as I had once done.

She looked at me quizzically. 'How many times have you been put on "disciplinary time", Nick?'

I laughed. 'Lots.' And before she could ask me what for, I continued. 'For doing everything from running a football pool to talking out loud inside my own cell.'

She pulled her chair forward. She was totally fascinated. Why had I been put on disciplinary time for talking in my own cell? she asked.

I told her that it was against the rules. 'But that's not true,' she said.

'Yes, it is,' I explained. Pennsylvania's penal system is based on one devised by the Quakers in the seventeenth century, founded on the idea that one powerful aspect of prison should be the mental punishment of isolation. Huntingdon also used the 'silence rule' for years as a form of punishment, although there they refined it further by designing the 'Glass Bubble' – the sensory deprivation chamber in which men were kept awake for days until they lost lucidity.

Maria asked me how long I had had to put up with this type of abuse.

'Two years,' I told her, before it all went whacky during the high influx of inmates in the mid-1980s, when mentally impaired men arrived who yelled and screamed all day long and no one could stop them.

She also wanted to know about the football pool. I told her about how postage-paid envelopes are a form of currency in prison, as they are essential to getting any help from the outside world. Death Row prisoners are fanatical about sports; and watching live sporting events on TV is perhaps the one pacifier that really works in prison. It keeps those men glued to their television sets for hours. I told her that the men also wanted to have a reason to watch the games even more passionately, and while I was in Huntingdon I gave them just that by providing them with a sort of 'lottery'.

Everyone placed three or five envelopes in a common pot collected by 'block workers' – usually non-Death Row prisoners – during meal 'clean-up time' when they came to clear away the food and trash. The accumulated envelopes, on each of which was written the secret name of each player, along with his choices for all sixteen NFL football games that Sunday, were then 'swept' calmly down the tiers of cells and under my doorway. I would then take out each slip bearing the name and selections of each man and put them on a master sheet.

Once I had them all in, I made a copy of the master sheet for each man, which was then passed back to him during Friday bed linen exchanges by the same block worker who had passed me his selection, so that by Saturday everyone had a record of their opponents' picks as well as their own and therefore could keep track of who was winning.

It was a simple system whereby I paid myself ten per cent of the total pot collected from the forty or so men on Death Row who played the football pool each week. Some men could afford to play two or three chances per week over a sixteen-week-long season and sometimes the pot got very sizeable. Soon I had gathered hundreds of envelopes in which to put my letters asking for help from campaigning organisations or laboratories conducting DNA testing.

Maria wanted to know if it was possible to cheat in my game. I told her no, as every man had his own copy of the master sheet bearing everyone else's selections and everyone knew that whoever had played a ticket with the name 'BDown' or 'DB' or whatever name had won. A tiebreaker was determined by whoever picked the closest number to the total score of the last game played that week. All I'd done was use the sports obsession of these men to help me get what I wanted without having to rely on others.

Unfortunately, my little empire collapsed when I got caught with the master sheets before I could pass them out. A team of officers found them during a random cell search. They took 300 envelopes of mine and another 250 for the pot that week. I was not happy that I had lost so much, but it was the risk I took for trying to 'hustle'. 'Besides,' I said, 'doing the ninety days of disciplinary time I received for this was not all bad. I still had my "Death Row doughnuts" to keep me going!' She shook her head.

She had no idea what I was talking about. I would tell her about that one later.

But part of the reason why I was telling Maria all this was because I wanted to show her how I was able to live and grow amongst all the ugliness. And the more I talked about daily life in prison, the more struck she was by how, as in any confined society, the men fell into a sort of 'normality'. No one can live in a state of constant terror, so after a while you just go back to living, period. How else do soldiers sleep on the battlefield?

'But what did you *do* during those ninety days of disciplinary time?' she pursued.

I shook my head at the memory. 'You were totally at the mercy of the guards running the so-called "Death Row library", remember? The simple act of asking for books could be a nightmare.'

I went on: 'When I was in Huntingdon the guards on B-Block were picked for their brutality, not their brains, and you could get stuck in some bad situations.' I told her the true story of what had happened to me so that she could appreciate what it was like to have weeks ahead of you with nothing to read and nothing else to do to relieve the boredom.

The guard who distributed the books followed a simple system. Inmates put in a request for two books per week on Thursdays, and these were given out the following Sunday, when the guard would sift through all the request forms and assign books to each cell for the week. If you moved cells during the week, then tough, the books stayed in the cell. They cared about the books, not you.

Now, the guard running the library was low down on the seniority scale as it was a tedious job to log all the books into the master folder. He also had to keep records of the books that had been collected.

Usually he did not care too much what he gave you; he just reached into a crate of books dumped in an unused cell and stacked them in a large pile two at a time, a little bit of paper taped to the top book of each pair. He used the simplest of systems to keep track of the books. Each was numbered individually, so he would write down, for instance, 'Cell 334: books given: 236, 421' on the sheet and then the turn-in-by date over the numbers of the books.

On the form that we used to request books, there was a small box in which we could put our preference for one of two choices: fiction or non-fiction. But I did not stick to just this narrow choice. Oh no. I had to go and make trouble for myself. All because I used that one fancy word: 'espionage'.

I was sitting on my bed one Sunday morning waiting for my library books to be delivered. I was serving my disciplinary time for the football pool and I had been placed in one of the cells high up on the sixth tier, used not only for men such as myself but also for some of the mentally deranged inmates. These men often did such things as pack the cracks of their cell walls with rancid butter in order to fight off evil spirits. Summer was the worst. There were hundreds of flies in Huntingdon, which thrived in the humid, sweltering conditions where insane prisoners threw faeces at the nurses who were trying to medicate them.

Anyway, along came the guard, walking backwards, with an inmate holding a piece of wood three feet long by two feet wide, piled up with books, and stopped at my door. I watched as he carefully picked up my two new books for the week and pushed them through my 'pie hole'. I went over to the door and picked them up. But as soon as I saw them, I called for the guard to stop. The books were in Spanish.

'Excuse me, officer, I can't read these books!'

He replied: 'Hold on, hold on. Let me get the slip out.'

Then, having checked it, and with an annoyed look, he said, 'What the hell do you mean, you can't read them books I gave you? I got your slip right here.'

'I know you have it, but on it I asked if you could give me some books on espionage. I didn't want to end up with cowboy novels again like last week.'

The guard looked at the slip again before asking me: 'What's "espionage"?'

By now the nearby inmates were laughing and snickering in the background, but I tried not to feed into them.

'That means "spying",' I replied patiently. 'I want some books about spying, so I wrote on my library slip that I would like to receive espionage novels.'

The guard knew he was being laughed at by the eavesdropping inmates and so he decided to end it there.

'Look, we ain't got no Spanish books on spying or no *espionage* books as you called them. These are the only Spanish books we got!'

Maria and I had a good laugh. According to the guard, at least he'd gotten the *Spanish* part right, so I could just shut up!

Maria could not resist adding to the tale by asking how my Spanish was coming along these days. We snickered at the ridiculousness of it all. And once she had stopped laughing about that one she made me tell her how I became the doughnut magnate of Death Row.

I pretended to dust imaginary powdered sugar from my fingertips as if I had just popped the last bit of doughnut in my mouth. 'Let me tell you about "Lifers' packages", honey!'

She groaned at what this could only mean . . .

In my efforts to come up with ways of funding my appeal case, I sold my services as jailhouse lawyer to some of the men on Death Row.

Word had gotten round that I did nearly all my own legal filing and I had built up a good reputation for helping other men with legal matters. For my first client, I wrote a mock brief for his appeal, which he sent to his lawyers to follow. Although I say it myself, it was well researched and well written. About a year later he had his sentence commuted to life without parole and he was sent out into the general population. Then, out of the fifteen or sixteen briefs I was involved in, another man also had his sentence reduced to life. Both these men were housed on D-Block, just next door to B-Block. It was great to feel that two men had been spared the endless solitary of Death Row due partly to my efforts. And they rewarded me with a monthly treat.

Everyone who was a 'lifer' was allowed to join what was called the 'lifers' organisation'. This allowed them to participate in lifer-only programmes, the most important of which to most of them was the monthly food package. Every month, lifers were allowed to order in from outside a simple array of everyday foods sold in fast-food places. One of these was a local doughnut shop, Dunk-n-Donuts.

Each lifer could purchase a set amount of food, which he was expected to consume quickly. I was only after one thing: powdered-sugar ring doughnuts. I asked each of the former Death Row men to hook me up with a box of doughnuts, which they happily arranged to have passed to me through the shower room door that connected D-Block to B-Block. I paid the B-Block worker two doughnuts for bringing them to me. I then sold twenty of the doughnuts to other Death Row inmates at the rate of ten postage-paid envelopes a doughnut. With each envelope costing twenty-seven cents, I made a nice pile of postage-paid envelopes each month.

All Maria wanted to know, though, was: Why *powdered-sugar* doughnuts? Why not chocolate or glazed?

Simple. When you wrapped each doughnut up in toilet tissue in order for the block worker to distribute it secretly in what looked like a normal newspaper, you didn't want anything that would get all smeared on the paper. The white powdered sugar also helped keep the doughnuts dry. I explained finally that, as long as I paid the worker some envelopes for passing out the food on top of the two fresh doughnuts a week, I was set.

Maria just could not get her head around all the planning and organisation involved. But I told her simply, 'Prison is its own world, a strange little society run by a weird set of rules.' I was just doing all I could to stay ahead of the game.

18 Singing 'Greene Acres is the place to be!'

I was transferred to SCI-Greene County prison in March 1998. The 'SCI' stands for State Correctional Institute, but there was nothing correctional about this prison.

Only opened in 1993 and filled with huge, hushed corridors which lead deep into a maze of housing wings full of prison cells, it is designed to break you down mentally. A man can spend years inside his cell here and never see another inmate, as prisoners are purposefully kept isolated from one another. Inside the normal Restricted Housing Unit (RHU) was also the dreaded SMU; that is, Special Management Unit, used for the most violent or out-of-control men. Greene has one of only two such units in Pennsylvania.

In 1998 Greene County prison was home to nearly 200 Death Row men. I was sent there for my own protection against further abuse by the guard Double D and, despite its reputation, I was glad to be there. It was staffed largely by former Huntingdon guards, whom I knew already. A lot of the good ones from Huntingdon had now been promoted to some of the more senior ranks here and I had no problem with them.

Just before I arrived, though, the Superintendent at Greene had been forced to resign. A former captain from Huntingdon who had gone power crazy once he had been placed in charge of a whole prison, he had been dismissed for ordering that Death Row prisoners should have all personal possessions removed from their cells and shipped home at their own expense. The entire Death Row population had gone on hunger strike as a result. Since I was not associated with this in any way, the Greene administration regarded me very positively, as a long-term prisoner with a quiet disposition and an easy-going manner.

Sitting in the rear of the prison van as we drove up to the front entrance of Greene County prison, I was astonished by its appearance. All that can be seen from the roads nearby are acres of land surrounded by what looks like a million dollars' worth of razor wire rolled between two twelve-foot-high perimeter fences. Only when you get inside the fences do you begin to realise how big this place really is. The main building is a huge sandstone bunker in which there is the 'control unit', rising above the surrounding 'spokes' of the housing units. It reminds me of some sort of school that had once been open to the public, but then they went crazy with the razor wire and cocooned it within this glistening metal boundary, trapping all the occupants inside.

Having been searched and having had my property sifted through by the intake officers, I was placed on H-Block along with the rest of the Death Row men. Soon afterwards, the block lieutenant called for me to be brought to his office. I was taken there by the duty sergeant – an African-American man named AJ – and two regular guards and told to sit in a chair while the sergeant removed my handcuffs, which had been threaded through a metal loop sewn into the thick leather belt strapped around my waist. Then the three of them took up their places behind me.

The lieutenant, Mr Fisher, who everyone called 'Fuzzy' because of his bushy ginger beard, was already seated at his desk opposite. He waited for me to get settled before saying hello. I had known this man since I was twenty-one years old. Now he was looking at what nearly eighteen years of solitary confinement had done to me. Maybe five years had passed since we had seen each other last and as we sat there talking I think we both measured the effects that prison had had on us. The lines on our faces and the grey hairs showed so many truths.

Fuzzy was a memorable character who had been in the system a long time. Mostly it was only the real 'country boys' who still wore beards like his as, following the explosion in the prison population in the 1980s, they had hired many new guards right out of the military, most of whom were clean-shaven. Fuzzy was 'country', but he was also college-educated. He had achieved his rank the hard way, through determination and education – most men from his background never climbed above the rank of sergeant – and I respected him for that.

Fuzzy had my 'jacket' – that is, my prison records – opened in front of him.

'I see here that you filed a request to come here after an incident in which you were injured. Care to elaborate?' he asked.

But I just sat there and said nothing, staring at his desktop over the thick frame of my eyeglasses.

He continued, 'Do you think you can handle being around staff without wanting to take revenge for the past?'

I looked at him as if it hurt me he even had to ask that question, before I nodded silently.

Next he leaned back, as if thinking about something, sat forward again and started: 'We don't want to know what happened at Pittsburgh and you don't want to know what happened here last month before you got here. As far as we are concerned you can start clean here and you can do that by answering me one question.'

When I asked him what that question was, AJ spoke up from over my shoulder, 'You want a job?'

I turned around to look up at him, but he was not smiling, just looking at me in a sort of neutral manner. So I turned back to the lieutenant. 'I'm not gonna be a rat, I'm telling you that right off!'

Fuzzy assured me they were not trying to recruit me as an informant. They just wanted me to come out of my cell after breakfast every day to clean up the food spills and sweep the unit, and the same again after lunch. I would be supervised by a guard at all times. In exchange for these and other janitorial acts I would be paid seventeen cents an hour plus any leftover food. I was also allowed to have a shower daily instead of the usual three times a week. For me, to be given the chance to have my door open for a couple of hours a day as I swept up dirty floors or cleaned and scrubbed filthy showers was a blessing. I would have done it without pay for the luxury of taking a nice long shower each day. It was a bonus, too, that I was allowed to pick through the leftover food and provide myself with better nourishment. I gave my word to the lieutenant that if they let me out of my cell without restraints I would not harm anyone. I couldn't wait to see Maria on her next visit and tell her that I was now in the food service and maintenance profession all wrapped up into one!

I lay on my new bed in my new cell and it all seemed so clinical. H-Block was made up of endless corridors of identical cells with identical ventilation systems and identical sealed windows, each with a solid metal door and gleaming thick security glass within cinderblock walls. I was curious to find out what it felt like to be out of my cell without handcuffs. I had lived in such poor conditions for such a long time that I even wondered if I could handle being out of my cell at all, with all the pressures that having an inmate job brings.

It is not easy emotionally to be a worker. You go from being in permanent solitary confinement to becoming a pseudo-caregiver to your fellow Death Row prisoners. As soon as the guards open your door with the push of a remote-control button, the other inmates know it. They all come to the windows of their cells to watch you do your menial work. They hate seeing you out there while they are still locked up; some think that anyone who is allowed to come out to clean up must be a turncoat. But I saw it as an opportunity. I had nothing in common with these men who had murdered others; I was there until I went home or died, period. Still, the disdainful looks on their faces bothered me. Clearly, they wanted to make me feel low for having this bit of 'freedom' that they themselves would have jumped at given the chance.

The unit contained two floors of cells linked by a short flight of steps. It was all fairly open and from the front entrance you could see all thirty-two cells. Having opened my cell door remotely, a guard would enter the unit and point to the broom and mop. He was supposed to stand five feet away from me at all times as I cleaned up the dirt and dust and food, but he had no desire to walk slowly beside me as I swept and then mopped a floor the size of an auditorium. Instead, he would go and read his newspaper in a small glass-fronted room fitted with a metal table and stools. It was meant to be a recreation room for inmates to play board games in, but since everyone was locked up twenty-three hours a day, it lay unused.

After I had done with the floor the guard would leave out cleansers and rags for me to scrub the four shower stalls, which were phone-booth-sized metal enclosures with spigots fitted with showerheads poking out of the back wall. Having opened the shower doors for me, he would go back to reading his paper and drinking his coffee. After I'd finished both jobs – which were expected to take two hours altogether – I was allowed to 'swag'.

That is, I could help myself to any orange juice or coffee still left in the plastic urns sent over from the kitchen and I could also take any pastries or toast and jam or honey left over from breakfast. I hustled through my tasks in order to get to the small room next to the 'recreation room' where the food was kept.

The most painful part of the job was wearing the regulation leather-soled boots I needed for mopping. In the first twenty minutes of being on my feet I was in agony because I had not worn shoes for so long. My arches hurt from being squeezed into heeled shoes. Also, in solitary you are not used to climbing steps, so I was very unsteady running up and down the stairs carrying things. I was also very aware of the looks on the faces of the nurses and female counsellors (whose office was only twenty yards up the corridor from the unit door) as they registered me cleaning up with the broom or mop.

However, there were other, more mentally gruelling problems attached to my job. All the locked-up inmates tried to get me to pass notes and such to each other. Being caught could get me fired as a block worker, but that didn't stop them. They were always trying to bully or cajole me into doing things for them. Now, a bribe I would have accepted as reasonable compensation for the risk I was taking, but they didn't think like that. I hated dealing with these men who thought that just because I was let out of my cell I owed them something.

That said, I decided to be fair and pass notes for those prisoners who accepted that I was taking a risk on their behalf, but ignored the tough-guy talk of the younger men who did not know me that well. I had done my share of fighting in the past, so I was regarded as somcone who 'walked the walk' as well as 'talked the talk'.

Sure, I had agreed to come out of my cell and sweep up for two hours a day, but I was not going to be intimidated by their threats. Meanwhile, all the haters went about putting in secret request slips to have me fired, while the rest of them saw me as a traitor – even as they smiled to my face and continued to ask me to pass things for them.

If it were not for the benefits of extra food and extra showers, I would have just as soon not come out of my cell at all. In fact, within a week of starting my job I really did not want it any more. I was so used to my routines and I was so sore from my feet to my thighs from being out each day that I wanted to quit. The running around and the cleaning-up of those filthy showers was nasty work.

It was also nerve-racking to be out of my cell in the presence of guards I knew to be violent, especially when a group of them arrived on the unit to attack an inmate who had gone off mentally in his cell. As soon as I saw them coming, I hurried back to my cell and closed the door. I did not want to be caught up in an 'incident', and nor did I want to be used as a 'witness' by either inmate or staff.

In prison, being a witness – or refusing to be a witness – can get you killed or severely injured. I saw nothing. That is, I saw plenty, but, as far as I acted, I saw nothing.

The block sergeant at the time, AJ, was a Baptist preacher in his regular life. He would come over to the unit and watch me as I worked and we started to get to know each other. One day I struck up a conversation with him while I was cleaning up some spilled coffee in the hallway just outside of the unit. As he sat on a white plastic chair watching me, I told him that I knew the majority of the captains and lieutenants here from my twelve years in Huntingdon. When I mentioned that, he looked at me as if to reappraise me. Very few men lasted more than five years on B-Block in Huntingdon. I had just declared myself to be a very rare bird by this revelation.

For my part, I knew his reputation. He was the son of a captain of guards who had been murdered during a fight in the food hall in a prison in Western Pennsylvania many years before. Not many men had the nerve even to mention this, as the sergeant was an imposing figure who stood 6 feet 4 inches tall, barrel-chested, with a booming low voice. This, our first conversation, out of the earshot of others, made us almost friends.

I asked him if he was really a Baptist minister. He liked it that I had given him the opportunity to make his usual statement about Jesus Christ and tell me how I needed salvation. He hit everyone with this one before allowing them to move on to a normal conversation. I smiled to myself as he repeated to me what I had heard him say to others. I really hoped he knew my questions were sincere.

For him, he told me, there were three basic rules: he did not care what I had done to put myself there, as his only concern was that I accepted Jesus and sought forgiveness for my sins. Nor did he care what others said about me: he was going to let me show myself to him for who I was. Lastly, he pointed out, any problems, I should go to him first as this was *his* unit. I respected that. He played no games and he let no games be played on him. He told me that he hated working around racists, whether they were inmates or guards, and he asked me if I had a problem with non-whites. To which I responded, 'I was raised in Philly where I was taught to hate everyone!' Then added quickly, 'I think we all bought into that stupid racist shit at one point or another, but I have no taste for it any more. And after all I've seen in prison I've come to realise that no one is better than anyone else.'

He was quick to let me know that any violence directed at another inmate simply because of his skin colour would be treated as a severe violation of his rules and he would not stand for it. And it was not what I *said* about racist hate that mattered, but how I acted.

Next I risked asking AJ about his father's murder. Was it true that he had never exacted any revenge on the killers? I had heard that he had worked for a while with these men and yet supposedly had done nothing. His face stiffened as he gave me his standard reply. 'People always said I looked just like my father when I was a boy . . .'

Because he knew he was a good likeness for his father, he felt his best weapon for dealing with the men who had killed him was to face them calmly. Every time he saw them he did not do anything more than just look them squarely in the face. He wanted them to see in him a lasting image of the dignity for which his father was noted. And he carried himself with purpose and without anger because of his acceptance of Christ.

I knew he was giving me his standard response, but I also knew that *this* time he hoped it would be genuinely appreciated.

Then he asked me in turn: 'Is it true that you escaped from prison but after a month turned yourself in?'

To which I nodded as if to indicate that my innocence was obvious. 'I had to come back and finish my fight.'

As I went back to mopping the floor I looked at AJ out of the corner of my eye as he thought about what I had just said. We had taken the measure of each other during our conversation and had both come away liking what we had found. I told him that I seriously doubted I could have done what he had tried to do with the people who had killed his father. He responded by saying that he doubted he could preach to others about forgiveness and understanding on a Sunday if he had spent the previous week beating people up. He kind of shut me up with that one.

As soon as Maria came to visit me that first weekend, I filled her in on all my news. I was so glad to be away from

Pittsburgh prison, especially since I equated that place with my last days with Jacque. Greene County was a much easier place for her to visit than Pittsburgh, as well, as it was close to where she used to go and see her little granddaughter. The plan was that she would come and see me on Saturdays, on her way to or from her daughter's house. I liked it best when she came and saw me after she'd visited this little creature who held her heart so tightly, as I revelled in all the new things she had to tell me about her.

In a weird way, I found I was no longer hurting over Jacque. I was so involved in my new life that I did not have time to dwell on yesterdays. It felt as if all that had happened a long time ago, even though it was only last December. You measure time in so many ways, I realised.

When I told Maria about my being offered the chance to come out of my cell and work on the unit, she was obviously glad that my conditions had improved, but nonetheless she counselled me to take it easy. She worried that I might lose sight of where I was. She kept saying: 'What happens when you no longer come out to work?'

What did she mean? I asked excitedly. She was concerned, she said, that now I had been given relief from the endless solitary confinement it might really crush me to lose it.

I looked at her, smiled, and told her she was being silly. I even broke into a rendition of an old television show theme song from the 1960s, *Green Acres*. She was willing to laugh along with me, but there was worry on her face as well. She was concerned that I saw all the good things about this place but not the real horrors that were here as well.

I pointed out that I had done twelve years in Huntingdon and *that* was a real tough test. Besides, 'I got juice with the ones who hold rank here.'

Still, as she left me that day, Maria kept encouraging me not to take things so lightly. It was not helpful for me to go around thinking I was somehow 'free' of yesterday. And just because they let me out of my cell for a few hours a day I should still be alert to being hurt. I broke into another lame rendition of the *Green Acres* song as she was leaving, but Maria just turned away. She could not bear to see me so upbeat, cruising along on emotions founded on such fragile ground as a temporary job mopping floors.

19 'Can you read me this help please?'

When Walter Ogrod asked for my help, he spoke in such a timid and nervous way that his words came out all jumbled: 'My name is Walter. Can you read me this help please?' He was sitting in a metal cage used as the Death Row law library at the time and I was outside, mopping up.

Two thoughts came into my mind. First: 'I have dyslexia, so maybe I'm the best person to re-flip his words back into order so they make sense.' Also, because, like everyone in Greene, I knew what he was in prison for: 'This man is an overweight, unkempt, bespectacled child-killer who put a little girl in a TV box and left her on the sidewalk like she was garbage.'

I was mopping the floor out in the main H-Block hallway one morning and Walter was alone in his cage in the law library as no one wanted to spend two hours locked up with such a repulsive creature. There were two chairs bolted down on to the floor of the cage and Walter was seated on the one nearest to the door. He was holding out a law book to me in both hands through a slot cut into the door, indicating for me to take it. He was obviously having some trouble understanding part of the text and he wanted me to read it for him.

I looked at him and snorted in disgust that he would even speak to me. I had read about his case in both the law books and the newspapers, and I had no time for him or his horrible crimes. Also, I had helped men with their legal work in the past and the last thing I wanted right now was to take on another case. I knew I was acting cold towards someone who had been assaulted and such by other prisoners, but that was only to be expected if you murdered a child. 'None of my business,' I told myself silently, and moved away without even responding to him.

Walter seemed to expect it. He just meekly pulled the book back into the cage and said nothing. But as I walked on down the hallway to finish my work I could not shake off this strange feeling. The next time I saw him I was going to ask: Why? Why had he just accepted how I dismissed him when he asked for help?

As well as being allowed out of my cell and to have extra showers, the other privilege I had was the use of the phone. It was at the discretion of the guard on duty, but I could have extra phone calls if I did all my work quickly. I was so grateful to be able to use the phone a few times a week in order to re-establish my efforts to get the spilled DNA evidence tested. I can be a real dogged individual sometimes and, despite my own lawyers and others telling me to leave it, by now I had decided that, as long as there was a shred of evidence left to test, I owed it to myself to see that much through.

In a review of the total evidence, a lab technician at Cellmark laboratories revealed that lab protocol called for them to cut and keep a portion of the evidence they had shipped to California.

I rang up the Federal Defenders Office to talk everything through and all it had taken was one simple phone call from one of the attorneys there, Christina Swarns, to the lab to establish this breakthrough fact. Not all the DNA evidence had been destroyed!

A whopping ten per cent had been retained. This represented a tiny part of a very small amount, but at least I was in with a chance. And when she found out about it, Christina got on an airplane to deliver the evidence personally to California – this time we were not going to entrust my freedom to an error in packaging.

In order for reliable testing to be done, however, we needed at least enough material for both a test and a back-up test. There were less than 3,000 identifiable cells in this scrap of material. A match head would have dwarfed it in size. Of those 3,000 cells, I now had to hope that enough were still intact to be replicated, thus producing traceable prints of the strands of DNA that each contained. It was that simple.

I knew enough about the current levels of DNA amplification technology to realise that my chances of success were not great. But advances on working with badly degraded evidence were being made all the time. None of that mattered, though, if there was not enough material to work with. What else is new? I asked myself as I tried to pursue this.

That May of 1998, I tried to keep things simple. On my birthday, 17 May, I called home twice, ate some extra food including some cake from the lunch tray, took a nice long shower and slept soundly all afternoon. Even in jail you can become so exhausted that you sleep blissfully. Right then I wanted no more tense battles over evidence abuse, no more rollercoaster rides of love; I was willing to trade all that for just being able to coast along and exhaust myself through physical work. I was prepared to leave all the thinking up to my lawyers.

Maria decided to point me towards the one thing that I loved to do, which was write. She encouraged me to place an online advertisement asking for pen pals. We were not allowed internet access, so I mailed my details to the website manager and it wasn't long before I got my first replies. People wrote to me from as far away as England, China, Peru and Australia. By filling my mind up vicariously with all my pen pals' different worlds I hoped to distract myself from thinking too much about the current round of DNA testing.

One of the people I wrote to regularly was Professor Alec Jeffreys, the British geneticist at the University of Leicester in the UK who had pioneered DNA fingerprinting. I had written to him asking his opinion on what my chances were, based on current evidence levels and the types of test available. I may have lost my taste for fighting, but at the very least I had a friend I could turn to for the best advice. Never once did he ignore my requests. I was so grateful that such an important scientist was willing to listen to me. As he joked to me, 'Once you've done something like create DNA finger-printing, everything else that you do brings you down to earth.' You have to love a man who is that humble.

The weird thing was that the more I acted like I had given up hope, the more I wanted to feel hope. I wanted just to let the lawyers handle things for me, yet the more I tried, the more I got caught up in it. I started to dwell on what it would be like if a miracle happened and I managed to pull this off. I mean, I'd feel so stupid if I virtually gave up on the testing and it then turned out to work! I remember telling Maria soon after I received a letter from the lab in California stating that 2,000 out of the 3,000 cells were 'useable' that I had to remind myself what my research had told me: Forty to sixty per cent chance of success, no better.

I was wrapped up in just such thoughts one morning as I was cleaning up the breakfast tray spills when, on the tier above me, I saw a guard who was doing a head count stop outside one particular cell. I was standing under the opposite tier, near the bottom of the stairs, so basically I was in the shadow. The guard lifted up the metal flap covering the crack through which could be seen the slim features of the inmate – a middle-aged black man – talking to him. Then, as soon as he'd finished, and without a single word, the guard tossed the entire contents of his coffee cup into the prisoner's face and slammed the slot shut as the scalded inmate screamed in agony. Next the guard looked around quickly to check if anyone was watching before exiting through an upper-level door to the control booth.

Other inmates started banging on their cell doors calling for the nurse to be brought over. A few moments later, I was ordered into my cell by three officers who had come to investigate the disturbance. Once inside my cell I stood by the door and continued to watch as the three officers – one of whom was the guard who had tossed the coffee – stood in front of the black inmate's cell as he kicked wildly on his door and screamed in some Afro-Caribbean language. When he saw the guard who had scalded him he went completely berserk. The two other officers seemed to tacitly acknowledge what the inmate was trying to tell them about their colleague, but all three took it in turns to yell at him to shut up. But the more they told him to stop, the more he went off. Once the guards had given three un-responded-to commands, they went to get the 'sticks and shields', so that they could enter his cell for extraction and forced medication by injection.

The prisoners in the surrounding cells yelled at full throttle as the three guards retreated down the stairs. As the one who had begun it all passed my door I looked him right in the face and read the name on his breast pocket: 'Graner'.

I had no clue who this man was, but I had just witnessed him not only burn the inmate with coffee but also become unhealthily excited about getting out the riot clubs and electrified shields.

I knew his type. He was an instigator who was happy to leave work having spent the day tormenting inmates who then went on to assault other staff who had nothing to do with the original incident. So many times I had seen defenceless staff be attacked for what their cruel colleagues had done. Graner was not a regular guard on my unit and I vowed to stay clear of him. All I wanted was to be left alone to get on with my renewed efforts to have that tiny sample of clothing DNA-tested and hide in my letters to people on the outside.

I would have gone without any further contact with this guard had it not been that the inmate whom he assaulted filed a complaint against him, citing me as a witness. I had no clue he had done any of this until I was confronted by a very angry Mr Graner. Had I anything to contribute, it wouldn't have mattered anyway, as the officer sent to investigate claims of abuse is usually a co-worker of the accused staff member. Which is what happened here. The investigating officer 'pulled' the complaint slip. But not before he had let Mr Graner read it and keep a copy.

I was cleaning the common area just beside the shower stalls when Graner approached me. The man he had scalded with the coffee had assaulted a 62-year-old female nurse without any provocation, he told me. As he said this I was filling a bucket with water from a small utility closet with my back to him. I turned around nervously at the sound of his angry voice.

As I straightened up and wiped my hands dry on a towel torn to rags for cleaning the showers, I suddenly felt unsure of myself. Someone yelling at me when I was not wearing handcuffs made me feel very vulnerable. Anger is a free man's luxury. Any prisoner knows that. If I hit him in anger, I would get time added on to my sentence, a beating and a year's disciplinary time. If he hit me, I would just bleed a little and hope he would find someone else to go after. I had managed to get transferred once as a result of abuse allegations; there was no way it would happen again. He could have owned my world.

So, I just stood there looking at him as neutrally as I could before replying, 'I don't know what you mean.' He then ran through the complaints made by the scalded inmate. When he'd finished, he asked me if I was a 'rat' whom he had to watch every second to keep me from running to the administration with each new incident. I replied that I was not going to get involved in anyone else's complaints and I was on no one's side.

He challenged me, but I just said I was staying out of things. He retorted that I had no room for error now and any sign I showed of being a 'rat' would be punished severely – as would my getting involved with things that were none of my business. I said nothing and tried to get back to my work. But I could feel him standing there looking at me and thinking about what to do with me. I hoped I was projecting the right mix of neutrality and fear for him to let me pass without further incident. I had seen how he enjoyed dragging that man out of his cell. I had seen the grin on his face when he'd 'stepped' on the prisoner's back as they had hauled him down the metal stairs. I waited quietly for him to act and then, finally, he left.

I did not have to wait long for my chance to talk to Walter Ogrod to ask him why he had allowed me to treat him so badly when he was seeking my help. He came into the exercise cage next to mine one warm May afternoon and sat down in the corner furthest away from me. I was sitting cross-legged with my back up as straight as I could make it. Years of sitting in bed makes your spine ache for correct posture. I was also on a regime of running around for about three hours a day working, which was exhausting me. I told myself it was the aftermath of the rocky times I had just been through, but I was feeling tired all the time and I thought this might help.

So, I was sitting there leaning against the exercise cage post, which made a nice firm support for my sore back. The sun was out and there was a pleasant warm breeze in the air. Sometimes Pennsylvania can be the sweetest place in the world. I was feeling too tired to do much more than chill out from the spent energy and gentle breezes that take your thoughts away.

Now, without intending to, Walter was making noises like he was struggling to breathe – I think his nose must have been broken sometime – and when he started doing this I got really angry for about two seconds. The noise he made was breaking into my emptying thoughts. Yet, when I looked over at him fiercely, he just put his head down. He wore these thick, dark-framed prison glasses, and his dark hair, which was uncombed and greasy, lay across his head at odd angles from where he'd been lying on his bed. Indented into the skin on the left-hand side of his face were also marks from the ridge on his pillowcase.

I knew he was doing a lot of sleeping, as he was taking medication four times a day. I regularly saw the nurse stop at a lot of the Death Row cells to hand out the 'little blue express' pills – that was the phrase used to describe the tranquillisers or psychotropic medicines some men asked to take in order to blur their worlds. We'd say that a man zonked out on these drugs had 'checked out' and gotten on the 'little blue express' to Rockview prison, where the execution chamber is located.

In the minutes that I sat looking at this man, he never moved. He was slumber-drowsy, sure, but he was also obviously on medication. His hands trembled and there was a white resin on his parched lips. He was over six feet tall and he weighed more than 240 lbs. Doping someone that size takes a lot of little blue pills. So I said to him, 'Those Haldol pills you're taking, combined with that Prolixin, they're making you too groggy. Are you getting headaches all the time?'

He looked at me a long moment and nodded before saying, 'The nurse is giving me something for them.'

I told him that, no matter what they gave him, as long as he lay in his bed and didn't drink any water while recycled air was pumped into his cell he would dry out like a prune. And if he just lay there all the time he was bound to feel awful when he moved around as the pills were slowing down his heart rate.

'I don't have a TV and my radio can't get reception.' Walter's reply was so meek that I barely heard him.

Now the reality hit me. The reason this man had allowed himself to be turned to mush with a handful of pills was because he could not escape his daily life through television or music. But I still felt no pity for him. He was like so many others – even the so-called gangsters watched endless soap operas and daytime chat shows, filling their every waking thought with television. Having spent the previous fifteen years chain-smoking and watching TV, one Death Row inmate dying of lung cancer in Graterford prison refused medical treatment unless he could take his television into hospital with him. He died a few months later, aged fifty-one, but only after they had given in and taken his television to him.

This man, Walter, just wanted something easy to rid his mind of what he had done to that little girl, I reckoned. I had told him that he needed to get off those pills, and that was all I was going to say to him.

Then another inmate in a cage across from us spoke up.

'Walt,' he said, 'tell him about the guys over on Death Row on G-Block who almost killed your brother!'

I recognised this man as a fellow inmate who had arrived not long before. I didn't know his name, but we were on nodding terms and he seemed friendly enough. I turned to him and said, 'You don't go to Death Row for "almost" killing someone.'

The man then crouched down to the same level as me and said in a no-nonsense way, 'I told Walt he should talk to you because you helped some other guys get their cases flipped on appeal.' Then he added, 'Walter said you ignored him when he asked for help with his book.'

I didn't like being called out like that; even on Death Row no one wants to act like they are better than everyone else. I especially did not want to give the impression of superiority, as within weeks of my arrival I had been given a job while other men who had been here for three-plus years just sat locked up in their cells.

'I didn't feel like being yelled at by the guard for passing things to anyone in the library,' I retorted. 'Is that OK with you?'

The other inmate was a young white guy of about twenty-five, who had committed a robbery-homicide. He had tattoos all over his body, most of them white-supremacist related. He kept to himself usually, spending hours in his cell drawing complicated pictures of dragons and bare-breasted women. I had seen the works of art he had created on his wall and on his desk when I was outside sweeping up. Lots of anger.

Walter spoke up as if the flow of conversation had not moved on from what he had last been thinking about. 'They didn't kill my brother, but they sure tried!' he said. 'He was stabbed over and over.' Then he paused before adding, 'My sister-in-law-to-be, she was the one they murdered.'

There was this pleading expression in his eyes, which got me on the defensive. I couldn't bear to look at him, so I glanced over to the other inmate instead.

'I guess you're innocent, too?' I said sarcastically.

The other guy sighed before replying, 'I ain't playing you, Nick. That man' – pointing towards Walter – 'is living a nightmare. Those men who tried to kill his brother are next door on G-Block and they've been grinding him up for years.' Then he added, before straightening up, 'I have been in the cell next to Walt for a year now and not once have I caught him in a lie.'

He stood up and walked towards the rear of his cage before turning back to talk to me. 'I tried to catch him like I was the prosecutor. Look at him. Do you really think he would make a good liar?' Then, addressing me over his shoulder, 'Do me a favour and just listen to what happened to him. Then maybe you'll see what I mean.'

Again, not wanting to become caught up in the misery of others, I replied sternly, 'I am not here to put anyone on trial. If you're so convinced he's innocent, why don't you tell me the story, Mr Big Mouth?' I knew he would stop walking then.

Kevin, as it turned out he was called, sat down cross-legged on the side of his cage nearest to me and addressed me face-to-face.

The story of Walter Ogrod began with the violent attack on Walter's brother Gregory in the home they shared with his brother's girlfriend. The boys had been raised by their lone mother in the north-east section of Philadelphia, in a rough neighbourhood, which had fallen helplessly apart during the crack epidemic.

Walter was neither a drug addict nor an alcoholic, but he had a low IQ and was deemed socially inadequate. This, coupled with his physical appearance, meant growing up was not easy for Walter.

Now, Walter's brother worked with a man who did landscaping in the area, and sometimes Walter helped too. It was physical work Walter was able to do, for a fair rate of pay. But one day in April 1992 a money squabble erupted between Walter's brother and the other man, Hackett, during which they nearly came to blows and Hackett left for the evening swearing vengeance. Later that same night he and another man, Spence, broke into the Ogrods' house while they were all asleep. Walter's brother's 16-year-old fiancée was later found dead from multiple stab wounds, and his brother nearly did not survive the attack. The police investigating the murder of the girl asked Walter to come in and make a statement, as he had been witness to the arguments between his brother and Hackett. So, he walked in the front doors of the Philadelphia police headquarters as a family member helping with a police inquiry and a few hours later he had confessed to the murder of a child, which had happened on his street several years earlier.

As I sat listening to what Kevin was saying, in my mind I pictured Walt walking into the police building. They call it the 'Round House' locally because it's shaped like several large Pringles potato-chip cans stacked next to each other. Hard to break out of a place like that as you're always going around and around, either up and up or way down, into the cells at the bottom. I had been beaten up in that place and I remembered well the copper taste of blood on my swollen and broken lips. I was not happy thinking that far in the past, so I drew myself back into the unfolding horrors of Walter's story.

Now, Kevin had all my attention by this point, as I really believed that he had made a considerable effort to separate fact from fiction. I also simply wanted to know what happened next.

The police in charge of the Hackett murder investigation had noted that a little girl who had been murdered years before, back in July 1988, had lived across the street from Walter. At one point they said to him, 'Did you have anything to do with the abduction of Barbara Jean Horn, the little girl they found dumped by the kerbside in an empty TV box?'

Walter answered honestly: 'Yes.'

He intended to tell them that he had once been questioned on the matter. But he never got the chance. As soon as he said the word 'Yes', the investigating policeman stood up and went to get his partner. By the time they came back into the room he had already told his partner that Walter had just confessed to the murder. Now he demanded that Walter repeat what he'd just said about killing the child to the second officer. Walter tried to make out he'd said no such thing, but they kept pressing him.

Eventually Walter made a confession. But it was like this man confessing to blowing up the Hindenburg airship back in 1937. As Kevin pointed out to me, 'Look at him. Do you really think that someone with a documented childhood mental disorder would have fifteen minutes of lucidity and brilliance during which he outwits the entire law enforcement community and cleans up after his crime, then falls back into being a retard?'

At which point, Walter spoke up. 'I'm not retarded. I'm just slow because I can't talk right.'

His interruption made me cringe as suddenly I realised we had been having an entire conversation about him without ever really acknowledging his presence. But he was not so much concerned with our pondering his guilt; he just wanted us to know that technically he was disabled, not retarded. I wished he would stop making that noise, though, as now I felt so ugly and shallow for having gotten so angry at him for it.

I started trying to show this man more respect as Kevin continued. 'Walt, tell him what happened at your first trial.'

In rote-like fashion, Walter began, 'They said "not guilty" to all the charges . . . then five minutes later this man on the jury yelled out that I was guilty.'

I remembered that the newspapers had highlighted another issue. 'I thought his trial was argued over the use of jailhouse informants? Wasn't there this guy they called "The Monsignor" because he'd heard more confessions in prison than a priest!'

'That all came out at his second trial,' replied Kevin, 'when they let the state re-try him for the same charges *after* that jury had voted to acquit him.'

I couldn't believe it. No way would a jury vote eleven to one to acquit a man of murder and then one juror rescind so they could retry him. No way would they put someone on trial a second time using a jailhouse informant to convict him.

Kevin looked at me as if I should be the last one to disbelieve that abuses in court happen. 'It gets worse,' he continued.

When I asked what he meant, he gave me a bullet-point list of what had happened to Walter in between the first and second trials:

1. Having his medication stopped after the first trial which then made him unable to talk calmly in court.
2. His mother dying while he was in prison awaiting trial, but he only found out a week later as that same prosecutor had withheld the information from him so he could not attend the funeral.
3. Having his fate decided by two jailhouse informants who made up a series of so-called 'jailhouse confession gatherings' to get themselves out of jail.

4. His only discovering in the courtroom at his second trial that the woman who had just died was his adoptive mother, not his biological mother.

5. His own brother running out of the courtroom at the revelation and Walter becoming so stressed that he laughed out loud nervously – which was interpreted as the heartless mocking of a cold killer.

By now both Kevin and I were fighting back the tears as the harsh reality of Walter's situation began to sink in. Then Kevin said out of nowhere, 'Fuck you,' before adding quickly, 'I never said I wasn't guilty. I gotta live with what I did, not what you think of me.'

I had to respect him for at least not being one of those men who go around saying the usual 'Oh yeah, I am innocent, *too*!' I felt bad that I had hit him with that line earlier and yet I was too unsettled by Walter's story to care.

Meanwhile, Walter just sat there, watched and nodded as Kevin recounted each part of his story. He sort of physically rose up and then settled back down again to the flow of the story, reacting whenever Kevin nearly told it wrong. I knew I was watching him relive each moment vividly. I have studied the complexities of human development and no one is that good an actor, especially not someone of Walter's limited capabilities. Now, sitting in that cage next to him, I realised that Kevin was telling the truth. But not only was Walter innocent, he was trapped in a mental illness far worse than anything I had had to overcome.

I looked over to Kevin and said, 'You paying me for the work?'

He never batted an eyelid before replying, 'Fuck you, white boy. Be like that if you want. I did my part.'

I went back into my cell from the yard, washed my face and looked at myself in the piece of metal bolted to the wall, which served as my mirror. It's like looking at your reflection in a blurry set of eyeglasses: you sort of know what you look like. Maybe. I knew I was being sucked into Walter's story. Why else was I crying now as I imagined how screwed up you have to be to sit there for a whole hour as two men discuss your every humiliating moment? You are so deadened to new hurts that you stay hopeful that someone will finally understand you enough to tell your tale correctly. So that maybe, after years of constantly being asked 'Why?', the truth will emerge.

I felt so ashamed that I had intended to do exactly what Kevin had accused me of doing. It was not as if I were in any way superior to Walter. I was a self-absorbed person who had had the nerve to look down at others while I myself sat condemned for being a sick rapist-killer. I never did ask him my question.

20 'Agony and misery both love themselves some company!'

In late August 1998, despite my best efforts not to get my hopes up, I was run over by the 'DNA Express' once again.

The 2,000 viable cells collected for testing were too badly degraded by time and exposure to the atmosphere to yield any results. I received the letter from my lawyers informing me of this the day I was sent back from the prison hospital. I had just been through a lot of stomach pain after a bout of food poisoning and had spent two days on my back being pumped full of IV fluids. That was after two lousy days in my cell vomiting up all the food and liquid in my system. Oddly, I found a benefit to being so physically overwhelmed, as when you are that ill you have nothing left for emotions.

By now I was in a new unit, on G-Block, where most of the Death Row men were kept. Sitting at the metal desk in my new cell reading the letter from my lawyers, I could feel my empty stomach burning. I sifted through the papers looking for the lab report – I had become something of an expert at spotting mistakes or incomplete details in lab reports. No luck.

By this time I had made a deal with Walter. I would write his letters to his appeals lawyer for him – thereby ensuring that his case was filed correctly – but I was not prepared to spend hours and hours writing briefs and researching on his behalf. I was barely able to keep up with the work on my own case; just reading all Walter's trial transcripts would have taken weeks. The letters back from Walter's lawyer were filled with sheer gratitude. Walter's mind could not filter facts or state thoughts correctly, and before, he had sent them twenty-page letters crammed full of unending sentences that made little sense. Twice a week for two hours I would sit with him in the library going over his case. Every time I went back to my cell thanking heaven for my lucidity.

My efforts to help Walt made me the scorn of some of the guards, who were petty, broken men themselves. Many made comments about the pair of sex offenders sticking together. Some dropped suspicious comments that I was somehow using Walter. They couldn't work it out. The silly inmates were just as close-minded. Either I was like Walter – depraved – or I was playing him for my own ends. I hated it. I had had enough of years of judgments being passed on me by both inmates and guards.

Yet, even though they bothered me, I tried to make a game of it and keep smiling. The most judgmental jackasses I have ever met are men who have themselves been convicted of the most heinous crimes imaginable.

The guards at Greene were a mix of rural men, who had a complete disdain for city folk or minorities, and seemingly more tolerant officers drawn from urban areas. They were rotated every six months to avoid long-term fraternisation and in June 1998 a new guard was assigned to H-Block. One of the locals, he had been given the job right after military service. A tall young man, dark-eyed and heavyset, with a loud voice and lousy, tobacco-stained teeth, he was openly hostile to many of the inmates, whom he viewed collectively as the city folk he hated. He was known to all as 'Lawless', partly because that sounded like his actual name, but primarily because, according to him, rules were only for lowly scum. His usual manner was surly – particularly in the mornings, when he was hungover – and it was his favourite inmate who had taken over my job as worker. I knew it was only so they could hang out and play grab-ass together. Every guard has his pet inmate they use to pass the time with. That's what happens when they become overly familiar and the barriers between inmates and staff lower. All you can hope for is that you don't get physically hurt by them in their rush to set up house together.

As soon as this new guard saw in my records that I was a convicted rapist-murderer who, even worse, hung around with a child killer, he set upon me viciously. I was fired from my job and there was nothing I could do. The block sergeant, AJ, said simply, 'I don't know what the truth is, but I gotta back up my men. This officer says he doesn't feel safe with you out of your cell. That is enough for me.'

I saw some amazing things as a worker. Having suddenly gone from being confined all the time to being able to walk past rows and rows of locked-up men sitting or lying there in varying states of misery, ignorance and bliss, the awful reality of the place sank in. And I learned one thing I will never forget: once they close that cell door, every man feels it.

It doesn't matter who you are, that cell hurts and it will scar you. You can read until the end of time, or exercise until you pass out. Whatever you do to escape will have to end at some point, and then, when your mind catches up with reality again, you will realise that it has hurt you and you will never be the same for it.

I tended to give Maria 'sanitised' accounts of what happened in Greene because she felt it all so keenly. I remember her freaking out when I told her how I had been asked to clean up after an inmate had cut his own throat with a razor blade he'd managed to get hold of during shower time. There was blood all over his cell and it had congealed into the track of the sliding metal door. I had to use a toothbrush and bleach to get it all out. Maria was horrified that I had been made to do this, but I reasoned that, having myself been placed in cells that were nothing better than public sewers, at least I'd spared the next inmate from becoming ill from the blood or bile left behind.

It's hard not to be affected by the alarm that shoots through you when an 'incident' happens while you are out working. And with 400–500 men locked up in the RHU of

Greene County prison at any one time, something goes badly wrong nearly every day. I was in the hallway mopping up when I saw an inmate smash a young rookie officer in the face with his handcuffs. The inmate was being removed from his cell by this guard and another officer for a medical examination. As soon as the guard turned his head and lost sight of the man's hands, the inmate hit him across the eyes with the jagged edge of his cuffs. But the two guards beat the inmate – a mentally deranged prisoner named Curtis – so badly that I nearly lost it. I was quickly thrust back into my cell and told to lock up. I was happy to oblige: I wanted nothing to do with this.

That inmate would face criminal charges and I was not prepared to be used to prosecute someone and then get killed for testifying. When the lieutenant came on to the unit to investigate, the sergeant told him that no worker had been out when the assault occurred. I kept my mouth shut.

Psychologically, I think that the acts of cruelty I saw aimed at other prisoners affected me even more than those directed at myself. Right then I felt more emotionally depleted than at many other stages in my ordeal. When you place groups of men who suffer from a whole range of emotional and mental disorders in the care of other men whose job it is to feed and care for them in cells, it is bound to produce the worst behaviour. Ever since I'd seen Graner toss the coffee in that prisoner's face, I had been on his 'hit list'. I thought I'd seen the last of him when I left H-Block, but no. And he reaped his revenge on me with mere words, I might add.

One day in 2002, he came to take me down to the unit counsellors' office to make an 'emergency personal phone call'. Such calls are only allowed when something major has happened: an inmate's death sentence has been overturned or there has been a family emergency. So I was feeling very shaky. The lieutenant had gone to get the key to the office door but, before doing so, he had told me that my father had called to say my brother had died. When I asked which brother, he cringed in the realisation that no one knew such basic information and replied that it was up to my family to tell me and he'd be right back.

As soon as he was gone, Graner smiled at me and said, 'For two packs of cigarettes I'll tell you which of your brothers died.'

I stared at him. I wanted to say so many things, but I could feel my head tightening as I started to shut down in anger. So I just stood there helplessly as he pursed his lips, mimicking my mouth trembling with frustrated curses strangled by my damaged brain. Just then, over Graner's shoulder, I saw in the doorway the lieutenant, who realised what he was doing and at least had the decency to scold him. 'I'll take it from here, Chuck. Why don't you get yourself a coffee . . . or some feelings, you asshole!'

Graner just laughed at the lieutenant's remark and left us, but not before deliberately brushing up hard against me. It was the cheap move of the bully put in his place in front of one of those he tormented.

The lieutenant dialled the number; when my father answered, he handed the receiver over to me. My brain was so shut down by my fear of what I was about to learn that I could only see out of my right eye. I held the receiver in my shaking right hand and pressed the back of the other hand against my left eye to stop the pain, which was so intense I could barely talk. My dad didn't even recognise my voice when I croaked into the receiver, 'Pop, what's going on?'

Then he told me. The previous morning he had gone down into the basement looking for my younger brother Marty as he'd sensed there was something wrong. He'd found him dead on the couch. Another victim of the OxyContin drug wave of the late 1990s. As he was telling me this I looked out of the office window at all the inmates walking by in the hallway outside. One who was being escorted by two guards stopped long enough to yell through the glass, 'How come they're giving that man a free phone call on a direct line on a Sunday?' Then, as his escorts bustled him along, 'I bet that bitch is testifying on someone! Get off that phone, you frigging RAT!'

I just dropped the phone into its cradle after whatever it was my father said to me. I kept conjuring up this image of my brother lying there. But I felt nothing. I could not even feel the pain in my left eye. I was just kind of light-headed.

It's the strangest thing, but all day I had been repeating to myself this line that Ernie Simmons, the Death Row barber, had said to me. Ernie was an old-timer who was the Death Row barber by default, as he was the only one of us with a barber's certificate, and cut our hair once a month. While he'd been cutting mine, he'd commented on how the old prisons were full of rats and mice, so that when you did time back then you 'woke up with rats in your bed and mice in your pillow case' because, as he concluded, 'Agony and misery both love themselves some company!'

I didn't understand what the hell he meant, but those words stuck in my mind as I walked back to my cell now. At least they saved me from bursting into rage or crumbling into sorrow. I couldn't do that. Not after being told how my baby brother had just died a miserable death at age thirty-eight.

I told Walter about Marty in the law library a few days later. I also told him how I used to be an asshole towards him when we were kids and that I had probably contributed a great deal to the emotional and mental problems he had suffered while growing up. Walter replied that he'd hated it when he and his brother fought, because it always hurt his mom and now he had no one left. So I shut up about my own sorrows – his losses were just as bad as mine, I reminded myself – and went back to typing up a letter to his lawyer, clarifying matters for the tenth time. I also went back to figuring out how to tell my folks that I had a terminal illness and that they would have to start planning for my death, too.

21 'I'm gonna let him fly'

In June 2001 I volunteered to take some expensive new medications to fight off the hepatitis C infection given to me back in 1993 after some dental work at Huntingdon. I'd only found out I had it when I went into hospital for the food poisoning in 1998, but not until new blood tests were taken in 2000 was it confirmed. The cost of these new drugs was to be nearly $1,000 a month for twelve to eighteen months of treatment.

Western medical philosophy in treating an infection like this is: 'Nearly kill the host and the virus will die first.' So they gave me a powerful cocktail of Interferon and Ribavirin. But I did not react well. I became lethargic, sleeping fourteen to eighteen hours most days; I had constant colds and flu; I lost nearly thirty pounds. My eyes looked like someone had punched me repeatedly and my skin became sallow. I was taking poison and it showed.

My pee smelled like the stale urine in a rail station stairwell. Everything I ate or drank tasted like copper. My kidneys had been permanently damaged by previous drug and alcohol abuse and my system became so toxic that, after months of agony, I went blind for three days. I told the staff they were giving me too much medicine, but they said that, based on my body weight, I should be able to handle it. They were wrong.

One evening in August 2002, I was sitting by my window in yet another new cell, in L-Block, thinking about how far my life journey had taken me. By now there were over 220 Death Row men in Greene County prison, spread over three cell blocks, in contrast to the twenty-seven men I had started with in 1982. It was horrifying to think how many people they were prepared to kill for crimes committed decades ago. I had the radio on in the background, as it was my only enjoyment – watching television gave me a headache, and, though my sight was back, my eyes ached so much I could not read. While the world outside baked in the heat, the vented air pumped into my cell made it so cold that I could breathe on the window and write in the mist on the glass. I was writing 'Adinoe' over and over again – the name of my childhood imaginary friend, an expression of 'I don't know'. Then on to the radio came a song, 'Let Him Fly' by the country singer Patty Griffin, which seemed to pull me right out of my thoughts. It was the third time or so I had heard it that day but suddenly its words gave me direction. I was not prepared to go through life in a cell in the full realisation that the life I longed for was not going to be. I knew what I had to do.

I had lived as free mentally, and was as well adapted emotionally as anyone could be, having spent over twenty years locked up alone in a cell. I did not want to die in agony from my illness and I felt proud of what I had achieved as a person, despite everything. But even I knew when enough was enough. So I decided to make peace with the world and say goodbye. After that very beautiful song had finished, I turned off the radio, went over to my desk, took out a legal pad and pen and began to write.

My letter was addressed to Judge James T. Giles, the judge in charge of my appeals, beseeching him to understand that I wished to terminate my appeals. I knew what I was doing: seeking to have my records transmitted to the Governor of Pennsylvania for me to be executed. As I poured out the words on paper, seeking to let go of my life, I felt so many horrible things inside. I was letting my family down, I was selling out, I was quitting. And yet while feeling all of this, I also felt so much compassion for myself and how I could stop my torment. I could be sure, one way or the other, that things were definitely over. Either I was going to die in their hands, or I was somehow going to change it all. I had no way to know this was the lone act that would set in motion my release. All I knew as I wrote the words was that I had suffered enough and I was done paying for what I had not done.

I put the letter in an envelope addressed to Judge Giles in the federal courts in Philadelphia, sealed it and placed it in a candy box alongside some loose photographs. The envelope was longer than everything else in the box, I noted, so I would be able to lay my hands on it easily, without sight if need be. Then I put the box in a paper bag under my bed and started making my plans.

I had a great sense that I was finally taking control of my life in a way that no one else had either the ability or the nerve to do. There were a lot of things to wrap up with some important people in my life.

I had a confession to make and I had a situation to deal with that would be brutal on both my family and myself. I realised that many others were going to pay for my decision. Yet both my heart and my brain kept screaming over and over: end this madness.

I decided to cease all medical treatments and begin trying to heal myself with just food and rest. And I knew that I would have to forgo helping anyone else, as I was about to choose 'the back door' for my own exit.

For by this time I had also promised help to the Death Row barber, Ernie Simmons. Sadly I gave Ernie back his legal work, asking him to please understand that I was just too overwhelmed by my brother's death and my own illness to take on anything else. I even let things go with Walter, as I was too sick to visit the library with him.

Ernie said that he understood and even made a joke about me being part of the white men's conspiracy to rob him of both his youth and his beauty because a black man like him was just too pretty to be set free.

I looked him right in the face and said, 'If I ever were to get out of here, I swear to God I'd come back for you.' We each made light of the moment, but he had no idea how much I truly meant it.

By that time I had known Ernie Simmons for nearly twelve years, but not the details of his case until we were housed opposite each other on L-Block and he began to cut my hair. Ernie had spent most of his adult life in and out of prison for petty crimes to which he had always pleaded guilty, but in 1992, despite no evidence linking him to the crime, he had been sent to Death Row for beating an elderly woman to death – something he strenuously denied.

Long before reading his case, I had a gut feeling he was innocent as in all the years I had known him he had never once lied to me about the case. And I mean not on any level. I could not say that of any of the others in there. That told me a lot about the man.

Back in my cell, I drifted into mindless hours of radio and televised sports and let 'time' go by. I had learned over the years to use this sort of switch in my head just to get lost in my daydreams. I could blink away a week or a month with very little effort at all. I still can. The only problem was that, after a while, I began to realise that whatever I was hiding from only acted as a sort of bridge to the bigger moment I was headed towards with each lost day. I could play my little game but time never loses.

It wasn't until mid-December 2002 that I sent my letter to Judge Giles. I also had this photo of myself taken, which I wanted sent out after my death to show what I looked like at the end. I knew that it would be a minimum of sixty days before I was brought to court to be put through a competency hearing, so if everything went according to plan I would be killed by the state in either February or March 2003.

The day I mailed out that letter, I had been lying awake on my bed from early morning. I was wearing only boxer shorts and a T-shirt, the air in my cell was brittle and dry, and the heat made it hard to sleep on the plastic mattress: you roll around all night while your body sweats on to the sheet, which then becomes clammy and wet because nothing is absorbed by the mattress. I made up my mind mid-turn to send the letter. I was feeling annoyed and agitated as I knelt down to fish it out of its paper bag.

Then, having stuck it in the slot of my door, I got back into bed and lay there, thinking, waiting, listening.

The morning shift officer finished taking the head count and then I heard the 'pfft' sound of envelopes being pulled out of thin slots in metal doors. I sat up in recognition. It was the guard collecting the prisoners' mail. I peered through my door down on to the officer walking along the tier of cells below mine, then making towards the far stairs. I nearly pulled the letter out of its slot, but then I went back to bed and lay down. I heard the guard's footsteps coming closer and closer, followed by the sound of the envelope being pulled. I'd really done it. I promptly went to sleep.

Over the next few weeks, though I was sorely tempted, I never once checked in that box to see if I had actually sent the letter. I left it all to this kind of make-believe chance, so that somehow what I'd done was not *real*. Maybe I didn't want to acknowledge that I had quit fighting and that I would go to my grave branded a rapist-murderer.

I often wonder if the other three men who volunteered to be executed in Pennsylvania before me had dealt with such feelings. The first had been Keith Zettlemoyer, who had been put to death by lethal injection at his own request on 2 May 1995. The first man to be executed in Pennsylvania since 1962, he had been in constant physical pain from the broken hip he had sustained after a guard had pushed him down a flight of metal stairs in Huntingdon during shower movement. He was also in constant mental anguish from his crime – he had killed a childhood friend.

The second man I had also known personally: Gary Heidnik. This man was insane. He'd held six female captives chained up in his basement, killed one of them and then mixed her flesh up with dog food and fed it to the others in order to make them super-fertile to his 'seed', as he thought that God had sent him to kill and then create life.

I was four cells away from him in Pittsburgh prison and I remember how he used to wait until there was a power cut – so there was no 'interference', as he put it, from radios and TVs – before performing this hideous rendition of the last hours of his victim's life and his power over her. In the silence he would also provide a simultaneous voiceover to his falsetto imitations of his captives discussing his own insanity. I still get a chill thinking of this man and his Christ complex. You tell me, how could the courts have accepted his word that he was sane and allowed him to be executed? He also died by lethal injection, on 6 July 1999.

I never met the third volunteer, Leon Moser, a mental patient who had been sent to Death Row for killing his entire family in a bloody shooting rampage. He was executed on 15 August 1995, before the results of his competency hearing had even come through.

These men's stories therefore left me with no real navigational aid with which to face my own chosen end. I did not tell any of the other prisoners of my decision, as it could make them suddenly feel very vulnerable. Death Row is a brutal, cold world in which men act as if your personal choice to die does greater damage to their survival than the fact that they themselves have killed other human beings.

My one major concern was telling my mother. I wanted desperately to tell her face-to-face why I felt it was better to die on a single day of pain than continue to live until all the suffering ate up what was left of me. I also owed it to her to tell her before she found out from the lawyers or the press. So I wrote asking her to come and see me before the year-end holidays, nothing else. What with Marty gone we would have enough to say.

I sat in my cell in frustration as the hours passed on the day my mother was supposed to be coming. She was driving nearly 500 miles from Philadelphia to Greene County and by 3 p.m. she wasn't there. I was upset, as visiting hours ended at 3.30 p.m., and I was just wondering why she hadn't turned up when two officers arrived to 'dress me out' for a visit.

Thankfully, I had two decent guards. I flew through the routines and by about 3.15 p.m. I was in the visiting booth. In the few moments I sat there waiting for my mom, I felt so stressed. And then, just like that, I stopped caring. What could have taken hours to explain would now have to be said in a few minutes. When she came in she apologised as she'd thought holiday visits went on until 5 p.m., so had left home later than usual and then got caught up in traffic. I said it did not matter, I was just glad she was OK. Then, 'I have something very important to say, so please forgive me for doing it like this.' We both sat still for a second. 'I made such an effort to be good for you, Mom.' We looked each other in the eyes. 'I have kept this from you for years now, but I have hepatitis C. I had some treatment but it failed and I have been diagnosed as terminally ill.'

She said nothing, so I went on, 'Mom, don't be angry with me. You have to promise to forgive me.'

'Forgive you for what, sport?'

Her use of that old pet name made me falter, but I continued, 'Mom, I'm gonna die anyway so I've asked to be executed.'

She just ignored me. 'You know, you really don't look good . . . you feeling OK, Nicky? I bet you're tired and you could use some of my cooking!'

Then she started telling me about this fantastic meal she'd prepared last week and how she'd cook the same for me when I was set free. But I interrupted her.

'Mom! I said I'm gonna *die!*'

She looked at me and, again ignoring everything I'd just said, continued, 'You look tired, honey.' Then, with a very forced smile but warm, tender eyes brimming with tears, 'Don't worry. I'll be back to see you for your birthday next May. I'll make sure I come early next time and we can talk about it then.'

The guard approached and politely told her that visiting time was over. I pressed my fingers into the metal screen in order to feel the tiny 'bubbles' of her flesh for the few moments her fingertips were held there. Then, as she turned to go, I brought my fingers to my lips and felt the warmth from her touch leave them as I pressed them to my mouth. They tasted of the chemicals they used to clean the showers with back on the housing units.

I had just hurt someone so badly that she had gone into complete denial. I wished I could have taken back the last ten minutes of her life. Then I realised that, now I had told the one person to whom I owed it to say that I was giving up the battle, I no longer needed to bow my head in sorrow. Ten minutes later, when the guards came to bring me back to L-Block, I was composed and ready to see my plan through to the end.

22 'Throw out your brown socks!'

After my mom, the first person I told about the letter was Maria, in January 2003. I had not seen her for many weeks as she had been on holiday, but by the time she came to see me I had not done much thinking about anything. That troubled her. She looked right at me and said, 'What about your family? Do they know?'

When I told her about my mother's fifteen-minute pre-Christmas visit, Maria looked heartbroken. I guess she imagined my mother driving home to Philadelphia trying to come to terms with the knowledge that her son was to be put to death at his own request.

We both sat quietly for a while as I retreated into that place inside of me I go when the sorrow gets to be too much. Years of suffering had given me this wonderful ability to leave it all for a while and shut down. It's the place I found that night after the riot when I saw those black, ant-like creatures drag lifeless, blood-covered bodies through a river of human waste. I found it the night I heard the man in the cell above mine hang himself on the last day of his fifteen-year sentence, rather than go home and kill his tormenting father. I found it when I had to block out memories of being forced to beat a man senseless in an exercise cage by the guards for their own personal wager. And I found it again now thinking of my mother.

Staring at me for a long time, Maria asked, 'Why have you stopped?'

I didn't know what she was talking about, so she continued patiently, 'The day we first met you were so full of woes and your hand was bandaged. Yet you were still able to face the future.' She looked me deeply in the eyes, searching for the person who had once been inside them, then whispered softly, 'Now you seem to have stopped being him. Nick, are you *in* there?'

I knew exactly what she meant, but I was just sort of done in by my own desire to end this misery. Although I did not realise it, I was mindlessly sleepwalking through it all, and I did not want anyone to point that out to me.

Maria continued, 'Don't you see, Nick? You have to live as if you have only *seven days to live your life*. If you had that knowledge, don't you think you'd owe it to yourself to live each one of them to the fullest?'

She smiled encouragingly. 'Now that you have control over the number of days you have left in prison, why are you squandering them?'

By then I was looking at my hands, cuffed in front of me and tethered to the thick leather belt secured around my waist. I tugged so forcefully on the belt that it cut into my lower back. I liked the physical pain it caused me, as emotionally I felt nothing. I didn't want her to see that I really did not comprehend her words, because I didn't want to and I didn't care. All I wanted was someone who cared for me to comfort me through my final misery.

Then she said, 'What if your lawyers convince a judge that you are incompetent? So many people have already hurt you over mental issues. Remember how the Federal Defenders Office made you submit to psychiatric examinations before they would pay thousands of dollars for DNA tests back in 1997? Nick, can you handle this type of loss to your dignity again?'

Before I could get angry, she continued hurriedly, 'If you don't go through with this, aren't you setting yourself up for the worst misery of all?'

That was it. I decided to ignore her. I couldn't face telling her all the reasons why I would rather die on my own terms. I was taking the coward's way out and I knew it.

I knocked hard on the glass window of the visitors' door to signify that I wanted to be returned to my unit. In the ten minutes it took the guards to come and get me I stood staring out of the window away from Maria, who quietly gathered up her belongings. I could not bear to see what I was doing to her. But I was done with having to justify myself to others.

I tried not to listen as she said a soft, love-filled prayer for me asking God to forgive me. I did not even acknowledge her as she left. Inside, her words burned me, but when the guards arrived to take me back to my cell, I showed no emotion at all. I was done with Maria and all her efforts to make me into a 'better person'.

I was done with everything, especially now that I would have to travel this last part of my journey on my own. I had already told the one person I had been prepared to fight for, my mother. How I ended my life was my own damn business. If Maria couldn't understand that then I had no need for her. I had her name removed from my file as my spiritual adviser and mailed her a curt 'thank you' card, asking her not to come back again.

Waiting to see what effect my letter would have on the person I had asked to schedule my own death gave me an odd sense of both fear and boldness. But as I sat there in my cell full of excitement and trepidation, Judge Giles did what judges in the courts do often enough: he ignored me and did exactly what he wanted instead. He ordered for all remaining DNA evidence to be tested, regardless of what state it was in, to finally find out the truth.

I was bitterly disappointed that I was being put on yet another DNA Express ride. And I was not at all hopeful about the outcome of this, the sixth attempt at DNA testing in fourteen years on the same tired evidence. I had reconciled myself to the idea of dying and I was angered that I was being denied that right by having to wait for yet more DNA test results.

At 3.30 a.m. on Friday 24 January 2003, I was brought out of my cell to be transferred to Graterford prison, just outside of Philadelphia, to be held there for a federal court hearing scheduled for 20 February. The journey from Greene County to Graterford takes twelve to fourteen hours by prison bus, which is gruelling even if you are in the best physical health. We therefore stopped off en route at Smithfield prison, built on the land adjoining Huntingdon prison, which acts as the central transfer unit for the weekly shuffling of prisoners among Pennsylvania's thirty or so prisons.

About twelve guards work there, processing all the transit prisoners in a unit made up of a large communal area surrounded by a series of glass-fronted cells into which inmates are sorted according to status and destination. There is a colour code system: white cards on the cell door for general population prisoners; yellow for juveniles; red for disciplinary inmates; and blue for Death Row men.

We arrived at about 11 a.m. and, once I had been strip searched and given a lunch bag containing a sandwich, fruit and a carton of milk, I was placed in one of the small rooms set aside for Death Row men. Relieved to have my chains and leg irons off, I settled down on my metal bench, trying to make myself as inconspicuous as possible to all the passing men who would see the blue Death Row card taped to my door.

Sitting there quietly by myself I saw over the window ledge two guards enter from outside, one of whom

I recognised from my days in Huntingdon. They were escorting a group of what I assumed were Huntingdon transfer inmates. The guard in question was a boisterous man with a penchant for jokes and known universally as 'Scaggi', as no one could pronounce his Lithuanian name properly.

I ducked down. The last thing I wanted was for this man to spot me and start his 'act' using me as its centrepiece. But then, inevitably, I saw his head with its greased-back hair peek through my window. I waited. I cringed. I knew what was coming. 'NICKY!' he shouted. 'Well, son of a bitch, if it's not my old pal *Nicky*!'

By then, the communal area was his stage and everyone else was his audience. Scaggi was the type of guard who went to work to have 'fun'. He would give a prisoner a complete strip search or 'dressing out' for a supposed family visit and then walk away laughing saying it was just a joke. He delighted in playing mind games with whichever inmate he picked on as the unfortunate target of his 'humour'.

So when he spotted me I just tried to look at him as impassively as I could. With his small forehead and thick dark hair, Scaggi looked as if he'd slept permanently on his face as a baby, as his eyebrows were so low. His eyes, set deep into his face, finished off the Neanderthal look – which suited him particularly well as his favourite routine was his 'caveman' act.

Ignoring protocol, Scaggi got the key to my cell, opened the door and told me to get up. I stood there silently as he made these melodramatic circling motions with his right hand, indicating for me to turn around so he could cuff me behind my back. Then, having brought me out into the communal area, he began walking around me and yelling in a circus ringmaster-like voice: 'Throw out your brown socks!' And again, using his hands as a megaphone, in a mock-official-sounding voice, 'Throw out your brown socks!'

Sensing that his partner was about to embark on a show which needed some help in translation, Scaggi's fellow Huntingdon officer joined in by asking, 'Who is this gentleman that we've got here, Scaggi?' Hilarious. I was in no mood for this. But Scaggi knew full well that I was not in a position even to raise my voice. He may have been a joker, but he was also quite capable of using his caveman skills to beat your head in with his club.

'This is my old friend NICKY!' he repeated. 'Him and me go way back, don't we, *bitch*?'

I looked at a spot on the wall above his ear. *No need to bleed over name-calling*, I thought to myself.

Jabbing at me with a make-believe rifle, he continued: 'Back in the "old days", my friend here was a real fun guy!' Then, pointing the imaginary gun between my eyes, 'Nicky, tell everyone how you used to trick the juveniles and other scared-assed inmates into throwing their socks out of their cell windows, *bitch*!'

By now Scaggi was half circling me again, jabbing the imaginary gun at my temple. I knew what he was referring to but I continued to play dumb. He went on to tell all within earshot how before Smithfield was built, temporary transfer inmates were placed in the empty cells above Death Row at Huntingdon. I would wait for the guards to go to lunch, then call out from the silence to these terrified inmates – who had heard all sorts of horror stories about the place – using an official-sounding voice like Scaggi's, 'Throw out your brown socks!' They were not allowed to leave, I claimed, until they had thrown their institutional brown socks out of their cells.

Now, with some pride and a whole lot of mockery in his voice, Scaggi proceeded to tell everyone how I actually persuaded a gullible few to throw their socks out of their cell windows. When I'd done my part Scaggi would go down the walkway yelling at these stupid inmates for being tricked so easily and telling them that any man not wearing brown socks would not be allowed back on the bus. Next I sent out the block worker with a broom to act like he was going to sweep up the socks along with the rest of the debris on the floor. Then I'd get these same sockless inmates to barter for them back from the worker with goodies from their bag lunches.

It was true that years ago I had come up with this lame way of scaring these transit prisoners who thought they'd landed in hell for an hour, but I was not proud of it and I was not at all happy to be put on public trial for it – especially by this idiot.

Then Scaggi upped the stakes. While still 'holding me at bay' with his imaginary rifle, he demanded that I explain to everyone why I was going to court. He said venomously, 'Tell them what just happened with your request to be executed, *bitch!*'

By now I was getting especially annoyed with his calling me a bitch and he could see that he was getting to me. I replied as robotically as I could, 'They found DNA that's not mine on items left at the scene of the crime.'

'That's RIGHT!' Scaggi yelled. 'This friggin' idiot asked the state to execute him and it turns out they got DNA from some O.J. Simpson-like gloves found in the victim's car.' Then, as he pushed me back into my cell, he said, 'I swear to God, when I read that newspaper article about this shit, Nicky, I felt a little bad for how I once did you wrong!'

Now, turning back to his audience, he paused for a dramatic moment before laughing, 'Nah, I'm just *bullshitting*! They could kill a hundred wrong ones, just as long as it ain't none of *my* folks!'

Everyone laughed as he went on to tell his listeners how I had once escaped from Death Row and how I'd then spent twelve years locked up on *his* block in Huntingdon. The way Scaggi told it you could have sworn he was almost proud to know me. All I could do was sit there patiently as he left me in the cell still cuffed, hoping I would raise a fuss, as he recounted the 'highlights' of my prison career. Been there and done it all before.

23 'You can't always get what you want'

I had no idea the next steps of my journey were to become so twisted. At my hearing I walked into the federal court only to find there both Barry Gross, the prosecutor who had sent me to Death Row, and Detective Martin, the policeman who had led the case against me so aggressively. I had not seen either of them for twenty-two years and now they had shown up out of nowhere. They were standing in a huddle with Sheldon Kovach, the new prosecutor brought in to handle my appeals on the state's behalf. Long gone was Dennis McAndrews, who had tried so hard to get me executed. From what I heard Mr Kovach was a decent man.

I looked over to see my father and mother's outraged faces as they recognised Gross and Martin. I smiled at my father and mouthed to him, 'They're scared to death!' He nodded, but I noticed he held my mother's hand a little more firmly.

At the hearing, the DNA results from the men's gloves found inside Mrs Craig's car were revealed: that of

Mrs Craig and 'Unknown Male Number 1'; also a second unidentifiable female.

Judge Giles listened as my federal appeals lawyers said for the first time ever that they believed I was innocent and that the results of the tests proved it. The prosecutor then stood up and interjected, 'Your Honour, these gloves were never entered as evidence, so we cannot now say that they prove anything. A jury never established the true ownership of these gloves.'

All eyes in the courtroom ascended to Judge Giles, who sat calmly throughout it all, high up on his podium. A middle-aged black man, his hair greying at the temples, he smiled pleasantly at both my lawyers and the prosecutor before saying, 'Let me get this straight. Is it your position that, because the state improperly withheld these gloves from Mr Yarris and his attorney prior to his trial, any evidence found inside of these gloves should not benefit this man twenty-two years later?'

'That is our position, yes, Your Honour,' replied the prosecutor.

The judge looked at him as a teacher might regard a student who has come up with a really lame effort. Then he looked at me before saying, 'Well, your position stinks. I am ordering that a final test on all known DNA evidence be made immediately; that further, both sides should sign an agreement that these tests, which are expected to consume the remaining DNA, will determine this matter once and for all.'

I looked at my attorneys, who had all gathered at my table. They tried to explain quickly to me the deal on offer: that is, in an effort to overcome the problem of degraded material, all remaining DNA collected from the victim's underwear and elsewhere would be pooled; also, all the spilled samples were to be tested as well.

Finally, after fourteen years, a court was ordering that all available evidence be tested one last time. As I sat there trying to absorb this information, I realised that my lawyers were waiting for my answer. 'What does this deal mean in terms of the gloves and the DNA we already have?' I asked.

The lead attorney, Peter Goldberger, who had represented me for eleven years by this point, explained, 'You have one roll of the dice, Nick.' Then he looked around at his colleagues and said, 'If these tests prove inconclusive, then you get your wish and we are all fired and you can do whatever you want with your appeals. But if we pull off a miracle and the DNA in the gloves is shown to match that of the sperm found on the victim's underwear, then you will be given a new trial.'

I looked around the table full of lawyers. 'What?' I cried. 'Are you waiting for me to approve this deal? Fine. I am ready to die, so what do I care if you want to put me through some new cliffhanger that hinges on yet another DNA test?!'

At which point I stood up, as it was time for me to be taken back to Graterford, where I was to be held while the remaining DNA evidence was tested. I addressed all six lawyers before me: 'Sign whatever deal they ask.' Then I made them follow my stare to where Randy Martin and Barry

Gross sat. 'As far as I'm concerned, just seeing those men's scared faces having come here to cover up their dirty deeds is enough victory for me today.' Then lastly and sincerely, 'Tell Judge Giles I apologise for my letter.'

On the way back to Graterford prison, I broke down; at least I now knew there was no more DNA after this. I felt like I could leave it all to fate.

Four months later, on 2 July 2003, Michael Wiseman, a lawyer from the Federal Defenders Association, phoned me at Graterford. I was sweating through the intolerable heat of the summer there and I was hoping either to go back to Greene County or have some news on the DNA tests.

Michael and I did not like each other: he seemed to think I was a rapist-murderer who was a pain in the ass as a client; I thought he was a pig-headed, brilliant lawyer who was wrong about me. Whatever. He launched straight into reading off the fax he had just received from the DNA test lab in California. The report findings were as follows:

1. DNA from 'Unknown Male Number 1' found in gloves matches sperm located in victim's underwear.
2. DNA from a second male's sperm, now referred to as 'Unknown Male Number 2', also found in victim's underwear.
3. DNA from 'Unknown Male Number 1' recovered from skin cells located under fingernails of victim collected during autopsy.

'That's it,' Michael finished.

'That's *it?*' I repeated. 'Don't you see, this proves me innocent!'

Michael Wiseman, a man who had reluctantly represented me for seven years, paused for a second and then said in complete and honest bemusement, 'Damn, I guess it *does* prove you innocent!'

He started to talk about how the lawyers in the office all considered me crazy for seeking DNA testing as most of them thought I'd done it, but I stopped him short. I only had six minutes left of my fifteen-minute phone allocation and I wanted to call my mother and father. Bye, Michael.

I was shaking when I rang my mother. After I'd told her the news she just repeated over and over: 'Finally, finally, you can live again, honey.' When I heard her start to cry I lost it.

I cried so hard that I had to be taken out of my cell and placed in a white plastic chair under the shower to cool down. I sat under that water for a whole twenty minutes, just letting it all go. I cried so hard I had the heaves and nearly passed out. I cried for so many things, but for one thing more than any other: that I had brought so much of this on myself. Having let my sorrow out, I wanted to leave it there once and for all.

Had I known that it would take a further seven months for me to be released, I would have spared myself so much grief-venting. In many ways it was so anti-climactic. First, Judge Giles ordered that I be retried by Delaware County within ninety days or otherwise be set free. Then my lawyers searched out Elliot Scherker, a Florida lawyer who volunteered to get my convictions there overturned. In September 2003 I was kicked out of Graterford and sent back across Pennsylvania to Greene County, although at least this time I was spared Scaggi.

When I got off the bus at Greene I was greeted by the top-level of administrators. Having congratulated me for being the first Death Row prisoner in Pennsylvania to prove his innocence using DNA evidence, they told me I would be taken off Death Row but placed in solitary confinement in a disciplinary unit cell until I was officially set free. I was incredulous. Why? Initially I was told that, as I had escaped custody eighteen years previously, I still presented an escape risk. But I didn't buy it, so I asked them to give it to me straight.

This time, at least they were honest.

'The things listed on your file that have been done to you – your hand crushed by a guard, assaults on you by other staff – we are afraid you'd take revenge. We just cannot trust you not to hurt one of us.' I shook my head and tried to launch into a tirade, but was hauled out of the room before I could do so. I knew it would not have mattered what I said.

I was taken to my new cell on H-Block, where I sat cross-legged on the bed. I had been restless and lost in my feelings before, but now I had a lot of new thinking to do. I had won but I could still lose it all. And I could be so messed up that it was pointless to leave.

Then I simply started dreaming of how my life could be outside. I knew that the 35-year sentence passed down on me in Florida for robbery would have to be reduced, if not overturned, as it had been scaled up because of my prior conviction as a rapist-murderer. I knew that the state of Pennsylvania would never retry me now that three separate DNA results had proved my innocence. I also knew that I had served so much time that no one could say I had not truly paid for the mistakes I had made as a young man.

In the weeks that followed, Maria came back to see me, not as a spiritual adviser, she explained, but 'just as a friend'. We laughed, and it was OK between us again.

'I see that mischievous smile is back,' she said. 'Does this mean I have to worry about what you've been up to?'

'Sit down, buddy,' I replied. 'I've got one hell of a plan to share with you! Did you know that the United Kingdom is the largest foreign investor in Pennsylvania?'

Sighing, Maria shook her head at what all this could mean. I told her that I'd had an idea to fight the death penalty using economics, lobbying countries which had themselves abolished the death penalty but which traded with Pennsylvania – and the United Kingdom was my first target.

'But first,' I said, 'I'm going to get strong, and then I'm going to be happy.'

Maria pointed out that I might like to find out what had been going on in the 'real world' in my absence before making too many plans about being 'happy'.

I replied that being strong and then being happy was a lot to plan for. After all, I pointed out to her how she seemed to have it all worked out. If she wasn't dealing with all those dying people and their grief-stricken families, she was out harassing soon-to-be-released Death Row prisoners, I teased. It was so good to look at Maria and see that, however strange our first meeting had been, and however badly I had treated her when I had wanted to die, our friendship had weathered it all and become stronger as a result. I felt as if I had a second mother there, witnessing my growth through my toughest days. Maria, I really do love you, my friend and guide, and I am so glad that you never gave up on me.

24 'Sometimes it takes forever to say goodbye'

Having spent an incredible fourteen years, from 1989 to 2003, without being touched affectionately by another human being, I was supercharged with feelings the moment my mother embraced me. It was like a physical surge of energy pulsing from her to me. I was so unused to being touched that I absorbed it like a parched man drinking water.

Friday 16 January 2004. My last official day in prison. This time it was finally going to happen. I didn't sleep much the night before. Instead, I sat by my window with my face against the cold pane of the security glass, trying to remember every face of every man I had known who had either died or left prison before me. I also thought about all the people who had hurt me and the ones I had hurt as well. It was a way of being honest with myself, I guess; of acknowledging that I was no better than anyone else who had been put through this same hell. But also that I was not the broken waste of a life they had tried to beat me into becoming.

I told myself that, as low as I had been made to live in the past, now I would hold on to what made me feel good about myself. I had grown in so many ways in prison; I even felt sympathy for my captors. Whatever justifications they had used for hurting me while I was being held for execution were no worse than the excuses I had made for my own behaviour. I tried to take a balanced perspective on everything that had happened to me, as otherwise, I knew, I would succumb to anger.

Even before that Friday morning, somehow everything had already changed. My next life was tugging at me – even though I had no clue how to handle it.

The previous evening I had been very close to going home, but the right papers had not come through in time, I was told as the door to my cell was closed in my face. So here I was, still inside the Inmate Processing Unit of the State Correctional Institution at Greene County. Now, in a new twist, I was being told that, since it was forbidden for any state prisoner to speak to the press (who were all waiting outside for me) while still on state property, I would have to be taken outside secretly. I did not like the sound of this.

Here was the deal cooked up by the brain trust at SCI-Greene: I would be driven out of the rear gate of the prison to the parking lot of a nearby hotel, where I would be allowed to meet both my family and the press, if I wished. The officer who informed me of all this was actually holding a clipboard at the time, which he glanced at now and again to make sure he was following 'procedures' – that is, the plans hatched by the prison administration in order to evade the press, who were getting increasingly irritated at all the delays surrounding my release. They were annoyed at being made to wait all week for their story. All they wanted was that one photo of me in front of the prison, and if there were tears, all the better.

Every day for four days I had been told that, after twenty-three years in solitary confinement, I would be released – only for it not to happen. So I was not now going to argue about how they proposed to get me out of prison. I had been through everything from the almost certain belief that I would be set free to doubting that it would happen at all. I don't know why I never lost my composure with each new disappointment, but I didn't.

On the Monday I was made to pack up and personally pay to have most of my possessions mailed out, only to be told later that evening that my release was 'not yet'. I fell asleep angry and upset.

Then, on Tuesday, I was awakened very early by the guards who explained excitedly that I was 'definitely going home today' – only for me to be told later that they were wrong to say such things without knowing 'for sure'. I barely slept that night as I pretended denial at just how hurt I was.

That left a quiet Wednesday on which there was no '*new news*'. I managed to sleep fitfully through all sorts of weird dreams in which I felt as if I were going backwards.

It was Thursday evening when my cell door was opened by remote control and I was allowed to go unescorted to the shower. Over the humming of the door's motor I heard the guard in the control booth say over the intercom, 'Wash up before you go home, Yarris.' As I walked out of my cell on shaky legs I felt like the survivor of a traffic wreck.

A mere fifteen minutes later, the evening-shift captain of guards shamefacedly came to my cell, saying, 'Sorry, but it's too late tonight. I have been told by my superiors that it'll be tomorrow now.' At which point, I simply sat down on the edge of my bunk in a clump. My wet hair was dripping onto my prison jumpsuit after my shower and my damp clothes were making me feel chilly.

My mind flashed to just moments before. I'd been all washed up and ready to go meet my parents, who had flown up from Philadelphia to Pittsburgh to collect me. I'd tried not to get too carried away, but when I'd walked to that shower flushed with excitement at the thought of seeing them, I'd gone around saying goodbye to the guys in the cells near me, telling them all how my folks were there for me.

The huge smile I'd had on my face earlier just melted. I was so run over emotionally that I could say nothing as the captain slowly slid my cell door shut without another word. I hoped he never saw the quiet tears streaming down my face as I thought how this place had crushed me real good this time.

How stupid I'd been to believe I was really going home, even though they'd taken me down to the Inmate Processing Centre that afternoon to have a new ID card made for me to take on the airplane – the plan being that I'd fly straight back to Philadelphia with my parents as soon as the court order authorising my release came through. The order never arrived. I did not sleep at all that night.

So, when I was told that Friday morning of the plan to sneak me out in a van, I could not have been more ready. It was almost like I was some embarrassment to the state that they didn't want the press to see in front of their prison. I even joked to the officer with the clipboard, 'OK, whatever you say is fine with me. Do you want me to drive the van as well in order to *really* fool the press? It's been a while since I drove, though!' No one laughed but me.

Four members of the Superintendent's office came to escort me from the unit out to the blue prison van. I said some awkward goodbyes to a lot of people I didn't know very well before walking through the door to the outside courtyard where the van was parked. As I stepped into the back and sat down, my precious little box of letters on the bench beside me, I paused.

One of the officers escorting me had known me since I was first sent to prison in 1982. I tried to make a bit of a joke about how he and I had eaten the same food for the past two decades, except he'd had bigger portions. The guards with him laughed awkwardly this time, but there were pained looks on their faces. With so many members of the press outside demanding to see me, the staff really hoped I'd keep my good humour during this.

So, with my box of letters nudging against my leg, I was driven slowly towards the rear gates. Waving goodbye to the staff as we pulled away felt weirdly normal. Then, as we passed L-Block – the unit on which I had spent the past three years – I looked up at my cell window. It was as anonymous as the rest. Seeing it then evoked no special feelings in me. One cell meant as much to me as the next, I guess.

It was very cold outside and the sun was so bright that I could barely see. I turned away from the van window and thought about real food. My head hurt as the all caffeine in the coffee I had drunk earlier that morning left my system. I was not used to being outside, either, and I was already reacting to the open air. For any long-time solitary confinement prisoners like me, sudden exposure to natural air causes headaches and sinus inflammation. I was literally allergic to fresh air, having been forced to breathe re-filtered air like a submarine sailor – except that instead of doing it for a few months at a time under the sea, I had done it for two decades in a cell seven feet by eleven feet.

The van passed through the first barrier, which slid down behind us as we proceeded to the final gate of the prison. But I was soon drawn away from my thoughts by the motion of the officer standing in the control booth next to it. He was holding out a phone to the guard driving the van. The mood in the van went quiet as we slowly drove the last few feet towards the booth and the driver leant out to grab the phone.

That's when I listened to one side of a very obvious conversation. Bad news. There had been *another* last-minute problem with my release! The upfront passenger guard, who was better able to hear the conversation than me, tried to pass on what was being said. Yet even before he started, I said over the top of him, 'Just back the van up and let's have this dealt with so I can get out of here!'

The driver and passenger guards exchanged cringes at how I had been literally inches away from freedom only to be stopped once more. The driver then put the van angrily into reverse and drove backwards all the way along the road to the exact same spot we'd left minutes before, in some awful reverse-motion replay of my release. The passenger guard even tried to make a joke of it by attempting to talk backwards, but I was not laughing now.

When we returned to the Inmate Processing Unit I was met by a new group of officers, including the deputy warden, and the guards hurriedly opened the van's rear door so he could speak to me. As soon as it opened, he began: 'Mr Yarris, I want you to know right off that your not being released has nothing to do with SCI-Greene or the Department of Corrections of Pennsylvania. We have been told that your Florida release documents must be taken to the state capital at Tallahassee to be officially stamped with your "release from custody" seal. The Florida state attorney has refused to release you from the order dated 12 January 2004 because there were no official signatures on your release papers.'

Pause.

'Your lawyers, who are on a plane in Florida at this very moment, plan to personally walk the documents from office to office in the Florida Department of Corrections.' Then he added hastily, 'Your lawyer Peter Goldberger is on the phone right now to explain all this to you. Please understand that we are not playing mind games with you. We are not trying to prolong your release date.'

I just sat there in the rear of the van, my legs half sticking out of the door, looking unflinchingly into his eager face. I waited a long moment before asking bluntly, 'How long?'

He suddenly looked confused. 'How long *what?*'

As calmly as I could manage, I stared at him a second long moment before replying, 'My mother and father have been waiting in the freezing cold to meet me across the road in the hotel parking lot, where you were supposed to sneak me over to meet them.' He flinched at the word 'sneak', but I levelled my eyes to his and continued, 'Now, I would like to know *how long* you think it will be before the paperwork on my case is completed and I will actually be allowed to see my parents.'

'A few hours or so,' he responded. And then, before I could say anything further, he added, 'Our office has already informed your parents of this latest delay and they have agreed to go get something to eat while they wait.'

As we sat there looking at each other, his features softened for a moment. This was the officer who had known me from when I first went to prison. Seemingly realising what I must be feeling, he lowered his voice out of earshot of the others before saying, 'What can we do for you, Nick?'

It hurt to have him call me by my first name, and I sank down deeper into my frustration as I thought about what he'd asked me. I was silent for a few moments before replying, my voice thick with emotion, 'I just don't want to be placed back in a cell, please. I have spent more than half of my life in a prison cell. I would really appreciate it if you would let me sit somewhere I can be left quietly to wait for this to end.'

He had that pained look on his face again, the one people who are part of a chain of command adopt when they are faced with something distasteful to deal with.

Then he shrugged his shoulders as if to agree to my request and walked back inside the unit. He began sorting it all out with the staff in the processing unit while I sat there trying to ignore the guard next to me, who was peering into my face looking for signs of emotion. The staff worked out a plan whereby I would be allowed to have an entire thirty-by sixty-foot room to sit in and have a coffee, or whatever else I wanted, while the state of Florida played out its last act of delay.

By now it was just after 9 a.m. and I found myself sitting in this large white room filled with boxes of prisoners' property. I kept aimlessly touching the boxes as I tried to shake off the surreal feeling of having been 'almost' released once again. Touching things seemed to help me believe I was at least awake. I had been actually *at* the door to freedom only to be jerked backwards. It was a door opened wide . . . and then slammed shut.

As I walked around the room I could smell the cardboard and the fragrances of the cheap toiletries the prisoners had stored inside their boxes. Then I sat down in a corner feeling really shaken, waiting for someone to come in and tell me the latest news. After an hour or so of no one bothering me, I let my mind ease a bit. Then I wandered around staring at the walls, wondering how many men had been beaten senseless in this room. The property room is one of the first rooms prisoners see when they enter SCI-Greene. Since SCI-Greene was a Level 5 prison – that is, a so-called 'Deterrent Factor Prison' (meaning the place you were sent if you had raped or murdered a member of staff or another prisoner) – many of the new inmates were dealt with brutally right here in the receiving rooms before they'd even entered the prison proper. Four trained guards with clubs can tear a man apart very efficiently in a room this size, I knew from personal experience.

Then, while I was being drawn into sickening memories of my own beatings, I started to speculate about what was going on outside. I was banking on the press being out there to stop the state from cheating me somehow out of my release today. Technically, I had been a free man for about a week, but no one had wanted to take responsibility for letting me go. I had even been mailed a newspaper photo of my mother holding up the front page of the *Delaware County Daily Times* of 13 January, showing the headline announcing my freedom. Except the photo appeared on the cover of the 14 January edition alongside a headline mocking the state for making my mother the victim of such a cruel hoax.

Then my former block sergeant, AJ, came in and sat down silently. He projected the posture of not inviting me to speak to him, deliberately ignoring me. Then, every ten minutes or so, another officer from the day shift also entered the room, said hello to the sergeant and came over to me. Each basically said one of two things. Either: 'I just want to offer my respect for how you did your time.' Or: 'I hope you understand that it was never personal', followed by, 'We do a tough job that hurts us all at times.'

Four or five officers came by to talk to me. It was clear that news of my stalled release had got around the prison. Since they all said much the same things, though, I wondered if someone had put them up to it. What also struck me was that they were mainly guards who had been involved in an attack on me a few years before. I let it go. Maybe they just wanted to clear things up while they could. No point, this day of all days, in getting overwhelmed by the battles of yesterday, I figured.

By noon it was just the sergeant and I left there in stiff silence. I was drifting into thinking again about what was happening outside . . . when I noticed the sergeant get up out of his chair. It was 1 p.m. in a blink. My mind was playing tricks on me. He walked over to where I was sitting, looked at me for a long moment and said, 'Did you *forget* anything?'

Although he said it loudly and straightforwardly, I wasn't sure what he meant, so I replied hesitantly, 'I don't think so. I have all my letters and stuff from my cell.'

He ignored my reply before repeating, with emphasis, 'Did you *forget* anything?'

As I fumbled with another 'No,' he cut in with, 'Good, because if you forgot anything in here, you'll be back for it.' Then he shook me firmly by the hand twice and left.

Now I understood what he had tried to do. It was him who had sent in those same guards to face me whom had once beat me senseless. He wanted to show me that there was something precious in this world that not even prison can take away from either prisoner or guard, and he knew that if I ever forgot how miserable that place was, I'd end up back in there again.

I really believe that I managed to handle my release as well as I did due in part to Sergeant AJ making such a point of giving me back my dignity in my last moments in prison. I guess I tried to show my father that same respect when I stood beside him outside the prison that day. I wanted to show him what AJ had shown both for his own deceased father and for me as I was going through that last hard morning.

A half-hour later I was asked to sign my Florida release papers, which had at last been faxed through. Having written down the address I could expect to be living at, as requested, I kept the plastic pen as a souvenir. I wanted to get something out of this silly, endless game.

This time, someone had decided, I would not be snuck out the back; instead, I would walk out of the front gates of the prison to address the assembled press. I walked with four armed guards through the front visitors' area, but just as we got to the last gate, one of the guards stole my ID card as a keepsake. I never noticed it had happened until later, because my mother, who was waiting in the lobby, made an impassioned cry and flung herself into my arms.

Next I held my father as he crumpled, saying, 'Welcome home, boy.' I nearly lost it then. Still, I had a mission. I stepped out to address the waiting journalists:

'I cannot forget the men still inside who are innocent. We now need to stop all death sentences in Pennsylvania and declare a moratorium on the death penalty here. I intend to fight for the release of two innocent men who are in this very prison behind me . . .'

I didn't bother to say anything about what had been done to me. All I wanted right then was to try and help Walt and Ernie. It was the one decent, positive thing I could do that day.

I could have lambasted the legal system. I could have shouted in anger or made an attempt to inform those responsible what they had done to me and my family. Yet the way I was released was so full of meaning and messages to me personally, that instead I spoke about my friends Walter Ogrod and Ernie Simmons, who still sat on Death Row. That was not the moment to prove anything. It was the beginning of my life, at age forty-two, and as I walked away from the prison I was wise enough to know that I had a long way to go before anyone would recognise me for what I had to say publicly.

The best memory that I have from my release was sitting next to my father outside a restaurant twenty miles down the road from the prison. I could not keep down food because I was still very ill, so as the others inside ate, my father and I went outside to sit and talk alone for a moment.

After he asked me what was the biggest physical change in society that I could notice right then, I took a moment to think before saying, 'Hubcaps.' I noticed that cars had gone away from hubcaps to fake plastic wheels or 'alloys'. I told him I missed the old style of car wheels and remembered how much they were cherished long ago.

He thought about this for a moment. Then he asked me if I was aware of how money had changed since I went away. When I saw that he thought he had one over on me, I slyly said that, no, I was not really aware of how money had changed.

He was so eager to show me the new money and the security strips that I just let him go on and on. He took out a $20 bill to show me the new holographs and security details to prove it all for me.

I carefully looked the note over while I pretended to be fascinated by his revelation. I then slowly slipped the note into my pocket with a big smile on my face.

He looked at me and asked me what I thought I was doing. I smiled at him even more as I told him that I was still his little boy and I was very thankful for my pocket money. He laughed of course.

Then, after considering how I had pulled one over on him, he had me go back inside the restaurant to retrieve my mother. Just like when I was his little boy playing out one of our gags from my childhood, he had me con my mother out of $20 by pretending that I was still not aware of the change in money since I left society.

I looked over at him as I pulled off the trick. He still loved winding her up after all those years of sorrow. You should have seen how alive he looked in that moment; it was priceless.

When my mother learned that she was at the receiving end of one of his silly pranks, she kissed me on the forehead and told me to ignore him.

I can still see them smiling together in that rare precious moment on my first day of freedom, and that was worth fighting for. I'm so glad I was determined enough and lived long enough to just see them smiling together over me – it's a memory I cherish.

We then got in a car and drove 500 miles back to Philadelphia, and away from my nightmare. I will never forget winding down the window and feeling the fresh air rush past my face – to the delight of my parents, who saw me finally *feel* my freedom.

Epilogue

I guess I am like any other person who has finished writing a book about their life. I really do not want this epilogue also to become my epitaph. Nor do I want the story in this book to be seen as a complete measure of the life that I am still living today.

A few days after my release, my mom sat me down beside her and told me very sincerely that I had a duty now I was free. She explained that for me not to be a nice man would mean a waste of everyone's time. I needed to always be polite and respectful for the gift of this new life. She then told me I needed to be especially kind and respectful to women because of the lie I told about Mrs Craig. She told me I would never stop paying for that lie, so I should pay for it with a smile and grace.

This motherly advice set me on my course of 'brain training'. It is a personal challenge and I have not had one single session of psychological counselling – not one – but each day, I have worked so hard to be super-positive and have thrown out so much upbeat energy and kindness that

I have managed to totally reshape my outlook and approach to life.

I have been blessed to become a father since my release from prison. I have love and opportunity in my days as well. And best of all I have found the meaning of my life in my gift to share my experiences through my writing and speaking.

The past twelve years have contained some truly remarkable experiences, which I never could have imagined when I was in prison. I have spoken before governments, major universities, and in national and international TV interviews. I love these events, and thrive on my ability to speak to students and adults globally about education and self-belief.

The one thing everyone asks me is what happened to Walter Ogrod and Ernie Simmons, the two men I promised to help when I got out. Ernie Simmons is free. He is living in Pennsylvania and has escaped his Death Row ordeal. Walter Ogrod still sits on Death Row and I am hoping this book and other efforts I make will lead to his release one day. It preys on my mind that Walter is still there but I have hope and I will never quit fighting for him.

For myself, though, that particular story is over. Although the DNA from the Linda Mae Craig murder case has been put into the DNA databank, thus far no DNA in the system matches anyone known to the police. However, in December 2007, when I settled out of court for the civil rights abuse and prosecutorial misconduct I suffered, I was at last able to say that my involvement in the legal process was behind me.

I have learned and grown so much these past twelve years of freedom. I will always work so hard to make my story one that is shaped by the positives, as I refuse to feed into the negatives. My soul, once poisoned by what I had been through, is no longer owned by anger. I don't need to forgive anyone for what was done to me – that is a notion brought on by ego. I know that my outlook is much more meaningful if I understand my Death Row ordeal as a toll I needed to pay in order to be a nice person in life. I was given a way to pay for all the wrongs I had done and I paid fully. I do not quibble over what was asked of me or what I paid. My rewards have been endless and my life so enriched that I hardly see what I went through as a loss.

That is my secret, I guess. I trained my brain and I gave myself enough education to have separation over what was done to me. The rest is just accepting what I had to go through. It has given me the chance to find a side of myself that I can love, and to share my message with others.

Nick Yarris
July 2016

Acknowledgements

I am truly grateful to Penguin Random House for allowing me to share my writing with you, as I recognise that the message offered from my story is so important to anyone who has felt trounced in life. I love that. I love that I can connect with people in this way. That thought takes away so much of the pain and hurt done to me.

I have some wonderful friends in this life. My grandmother used to tell me as a child that if I showed her who my friends were, then she could tell me who I was. I love to remember those words as I have found myself surrounded with really remarkable and soulfully open people. The many people I have befriended after they found me on Facebook or Twitter are much the same. They saw the film *The Fear of 13* or they read this book and they went out of their way to write to me and say hello – I really appreciate that.

My mother, Jayne, passed away in 2011. My father, Michael, is still going at eighty-two years of age as I write this. My parents were together through fifty-six years of marriage. The remarkable ability they both had for love-filled endurance is deeply within me now, and so this book is dedicated to them.